freehand machine embroidery

Poppy Treffry

D&C
David and Charles

www.rucraft.co.uk

CONTENTS

Introduction

Hello and welcome to my second book on freehand machine embroidery. I have had so much fun putting this book together and there are lots of lovely new projects for you.

I've divided the projects into four sections: Getting Crafty, New Arrivals, Party Time and Happy Holidays. These chapters seem to encapsulate perfectly the different themes that run through my work, so here you will find tablecloths, knitting bags, baby blankets and all sorts!

The projects within each section go from easy peasy to a bit more tricky but also go from a teeny scrap of fabric to a great big bit of fabric, so there are some great little projects for people just starting out and some ideal projects to make use of all that lovely fabric I know you're all hoarding!

So, pop the 'do not disturb' sign up on the door and get stitching…

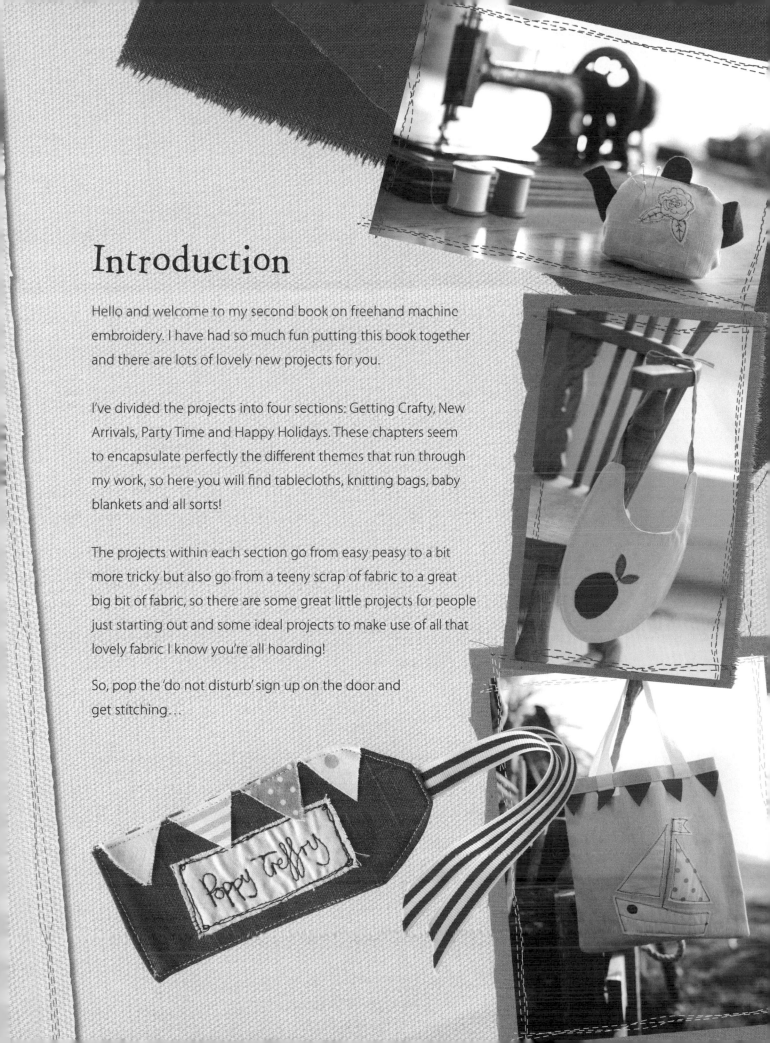

STARTING OUT

Basic equipment

While it's not rocket science, you need a few key things for success with freehand machine embroidery. I think the saying, 'buy cheap, buy twice' is definitely true here and good-quality equipment and fabrics will make your life much easier. That doesn't mean it has to be new though, as if you're a hoarder like me, I'll bet you'll find some great stuff in the attic!

Wooden embroidery hoop

It's important to spend a bit of money here and get a really good-quality hoop. Cheaper hoops may damage your fabric or not hold it tightly enough. Choose the size that suits your piece of work. A 20cm (8in) hoop is a very versatile size, but it's also handy to have a smaller 10cm (4in) hoop and possibly a bigger one too.

Threads in lots of colours

Good-quality polyester thread works best. Poor-quality thread will snap constantly and make your life a misery, though you may get away with it for winding the bobbin. You'll need lots of colours – I love grey, black, red, orange, blue, green, cream and white.

Sharp scissors

Again, good quality is essential for a pair of tailors' shears and a little pair of trimming scissors. It's important to keep them sharp – otherwise you make your work harder. So, no chopping paper with them!

Yummy fabric scraps

Collect lots! You want to be inspired by your fabrics, so make sure you've got lots of lovely little pieces hoarded for your projects. Use scraps from previous projects, your own old clothes or hunt out treasures from vintage and thrift stores. Heavy fabrics or ones with a loose weave don't work so well, but cotton patchwork fabrics are ideal.

Buttons, bits and bobs

Big distinctive buttons, and other decorative bits and bobs, are great for giving your projects the personal touch. Don't forget to sew them on with strong thread! And always go for the best quality you can afford – the better the ingredients, the better the dish!

Templates

In most of the projects I have given measurements rather than templates for the base pieces of fabric but the templates for the appliqué are at the back of the book in the Templates section. The appliqué works in layers to complete the whole motif so you will need to trace off the individual sections of the template.

Fabrics

Picking just the right fabrics is crucial to the success of your freehand embroidery journey. And let's face it, it's the most fun bit too! I love playing with colour and selecting a palette of fabrics to work with. As you get more experienced you'll learn to spot a good one at 20 paces. You'll learn to recognize the ones that are a bit too 'bouncy', the one's that are too fluffy or fray too much and you'll hone your collection down to the chosen few that work for you.

Background fabrics

These will generally be plain and medium- to heavyweight fabrics. Natural fibres such as cotton, linen and wool make great background fabrics as they provide a stable base. The best place to find suitable fabrics will probably be the furnishing section of the fabric store.

I try to keep my appliqué fabric box neat and tidy so I can find what I need

Top tips for choosing fabrics

- Is the fabric for the background, the appliqué or other parts of the project? You might need to consider different types of fabric depending on the purpose.

- Will the project need to be washed? Wash a scrap of fabric to make sure it's colourfast, doesn't shrink and presses well.

- Will the project take some knocks? A more hardwearing fabric will be best.

- Is the fabric for a picture or wall hanging? A more delicate fabric will be fine.

stacks of fabric ready
to become Poppy
Treffry products!

Project fabrics

Choose the fabric to suit the project. For example, an evening bag
will look very glamorous in light, luxurious fabrics. On the other hand,
a shopping bag will need a hardwearing, medium- to heavyweight
fabric – such as cotton, linen, corduroy or tweed – for handles, button
loops and lining. Make sure the fabric isn't too thick, though, so that
it doesn't make the seams too bulky. You could also add another
dimension by choosing colours and patterns to complement or
contrast with the main background fabric.

some of my favourite
stripes and florals

projects that use loads of different fabrics mean you can really get creative

I sort my fabrics into plains, stripes, florals and spots

I keep really special bits of fabric in an old cigar box

Special Scraps.

Appliqué fabrics

This is where you can have the most fun – using all your old scraps, cutting up worn-out old clothes and collecting bits from friends and family. By using vintage and used scraps, you can make your work more original and personal. Of course, you can also buy small amounts of fabrics especially for your projects, and most patchwork fabrics and a lot of dress fabrics are perfect for the job.

It's best to stick to natural, medium-weight fabrics. Synthetic fabrics may stretch when you are stitching into them or melt when ironed. If your fabric is too transparent, you may be able to see too much of your background fabric underneath and this may spoil the effect. If it is too thick or too flimsy, it will be difficult to work with.

Test whether the fabric will fray. A little bit of fraying gives a nice effect but too much and the fabric becomes unworkable. Consider the size of the pattern on your fabric. Big patterns will not work so well once the fabric is cut out for appliqué, so it's better to choose fabrics with small-scale patterns.

Enjoy building up your collection and, if you can get away with it, make sure that you have somewhere to display your finds. I know my fabric collection is what inspires me to keep on sewing and I hope yours will do the same for you!

13

Getting to grips with your sewing machine

If you don't already have a trusty machine that you know will do everything you want then choosing a new one can be quite a minefield! I am really not an expert on any machines other than the old Singers that I use, but at my courses I've seen my technique work beautifully on all sorts of machines. Many models will get to grips with the technique with the right knowledge of your machine and a bit of patience. Here are a few tips to help you choose something that will take well to freehand embroidery.

Key machine features

- The main thing you need the machine to be able to do is drop the feed dogs. These are the little teeth that feed the fabric through. When you are free machining it's you that's controlling the movement of the fabric so you need these little fellows out of the way!

- The next thing is the weight of the machine – I find it helps if the machine is quite heavy. Not so good for carrying it around but definitely good if you're going to do quite a lot of free machining, as it will stand up well to being put through its paces with a technique that is quite different to straightforward sewing.

- Another important thing to consider is where you buy your machine. I think it's best to get either a new one or a fully serviced one from your local sewing shop. Hopefully they will be really knowledgeable on the different machines and this will help not just in choosing a machine but also in repairing, servicing and providing general support as you get to know it and its quirks!

- Above all you need a machine you're comfortable working with, that you can thread easily, where the controls aren't too scary to even touch and that you know you'll get along with. For me, this was my humble old Singer. When I was younger I had a much more modern machine and I don't think I ever managed to finish a single item on it – I didn't quite throw it out of the window but I came close and I certainly didn't think I could sew. I realize now that it's often just a few tiny tweaks to tension, needle type and thread type that make the difference between a joyful afternoon sewing and a big horrible tangle!

Sewing machine feet

Those of you that know my work or have come on one of my courses will know that I don't use any special feet for my work. I simply drop the feed dogs, remove the foot and get stitching. That said, I know this doesn't work for everyone so below is what I've learned so far about feet.

• The preferred foot used for freehand machining is called a darning foot or a free-motion foot. You can buy various different types – some plastic, some metal – and they will protect your fingers from getting too close to the needle as you work. These seem to work well though I find some can obscure your view of the stitching a little so check that you get a really clear view before you buy. They can also be quite specific to your machine so always ask a sewing-machine dealer which one to get, especially if you have quite a new machine.

• Check that your embroidery hoop fits easily under the foot (you don't want to be taking it off every time you remove the hoop from the sewing machine).

• You also want to make sure that the foot does not grip your fabric too much as you sew, as you want to be able to move your fabric freely to get your freehand effects.

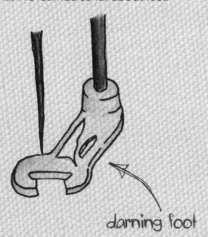

darning foot

Dropping the feed dogs

A lot of people don't know what feed dogs are when they first start sewing – let alone how to drop them! And why would they? Feed dogs are the little teeth that pull your fabric through and your mission when you start free machining is to get them to stop doing their job and stay out of the way (or at least stay still).

There are a few ways to do this. Most modern machines will have a button, a lever or a screw somewhere that drops the feed dogs and this should be explained in the machine's manual. But if they don't have this or your machine is a little older you have a couple of options. You can buy a special plate that covers the feed dogs. These seem to work well, but the only problem I see with them is that your work does not sit completely flat on the bed of the sewing machine and this could affect your tension a little but with practice this shouldn't be a problem.

The other option is to set your stitch length to zero or as close to it as you can. This way the feed dogs shouldn't move at all although they will still be sticking up a little so be careful your work doesn't snag on them. You could always put a bit of masking tape over them to smooth them off.

The more people I meet through free machining the more I learn about all the different ways of doing things. There is no right or wrong way of doing it – just what works for you. I'm sure before too long you'll be meeting up with other freehand machine embroidery addicts and learning a whole host of new tricks!

feed dogs dropped

Maintaining your machine

Your sewing machine will love you so much if you give it a little TLC once in a while. Use a stiff brush and a vacuum cleaner to give it a good de-fluffing. It always makes me feel like a dentist! Undo any screws you can and get all the fluff out from around the bobbin and any other workings you can access easily. Then you can give it some oil, following your machine's manual so it goes in the right places. I use Singer oil for mine. It's amazing what a difference this can make to your machine's behaviour! It's also good to put a new needle in every now and then so it's good and sharp.

Choosing threads

You could just use one colour for your embroidery, but mixing two colours will give you some great effects even if you have never stitched in this way before. Using a different coloured thread for the top thread and the bobbin will give your stitching a more artistic quality. You can mix them to create depth, texture and interest in your work – just like mixing paints. I recommend a grey top thread and black bobbin thread for getting started, as they produce a nice strong line a bit like a pencil drawing. Other favourites are an orange top and red bobbin thread, a pink top and white bobbin thread, and a blue top and green bobbin thread.

orange and red thread combined

black and grey shading

pale green/white stitching on dark blue fabric

tip : Keep a collection of bobbins wound with different coloured threads so that you can change and play around with colours quickly and easily.

Thread tension

Follow your machine manual for guidance on tension, especially if you want to keep it regular. You can also create great special effects by altering the tension. For example, tighten the tension of the top thread to let more of your accent colour come through or loosen it so that you see more of the top thread. All machines will behave differently here, so it's worth having a play to see what your machine can do. Remember that the tension will be affected by the weight of the fabric you are using, how tightly it is stretched over your hoop, and the thickness and quality of the thread you choose. Once you find a tension setting that feels comfortable, then it's best to stick with it.

Hoop up!

Before you start embroidering you need to stretch your fabric in an embroidery hoop so that it doesn't pucker. The finished results depend on getting this right, so don't worry if you have to practise. The tighter you can stretch your fabric over the hoop, the better your embroidery will look.

one Adjust the screw to open the outer hoop slightly.

two Place your background fabric over the outer hoop, right side up, so there's the same amount of excess fabric on all sides. Position the screw on the hoop furthest away from you.

three Position the inner hoop on top of your fabric so that it sits within the outer hoop. The fit should be tight, but not so much that you force the hoops or mark the fabric.

four Adjust the outer hoop to make the fit tighter if necessary. You will have more success if you adjust it close to the right size before fitting the inner hoop.

five Work your way around the hoop, holding your thumb on the top edge and gently pulling the fabric to make it as tight as it will go – a bit like a drum skin.

TECHNIQUES

Having a play

Having a play is the most important part of learning to free machine. Even experienced sewers will really benefit from freeing up and getting into the flow of the technique if they haven't tried it before. On my courses, I give people loads of squares of practice fabric and encourage them just to fill them up with scribbles and it really does work to get through those teething troubles and begin to feel more relaxed behind the machine.

Top tips for having a play

- Find some medium-weight fabric you're not too precious about so you can just fill it up.
- See all the snarl ups and needle snappings as part of the learning curve and completely normal!
- Don't, don't, and I repeat don't, try to do anything perfect!

one Thread your machine and hoop up your fabric. Drop the feed dogs and place your hoop under the needle. Lower the needle into the fabric. Set your machine to straight stitch and for even tension. The length of the stitch will be controlled by the speed at which you move the hoop.

two Start to sew slowly, controlling the speed carefully with your foot. At this stage don't worry about the shape, sew some wiggly lines and scribbles just to feel comfortable with the machine. As your confidence grows, increase the speed to a steady medium pace so your stitched lines flow more smoothly.

three Next try some simple shapes like squares and circles with the needle. You will get the feel for what the machine will do and realize that you can move the hoop in any direction.

squiggles to start

double outlines look attractive

Outlining

Outlining is the first step in freehand machine embroidery (after you've had a good old scribble that is). You can use it to draw with your sewing machine, to outline a shape to fill in with shading or as part of working with appliqué. Like everything with machining it will take practice and at first your lines will be jerky and very difficult to control – but patience my friend – they will get better!

one By now you will have done lots of scribbles so you can progress from having a play to trying some more specific shapes. You could try some from the projects in the book like the fruit from the Summer Fruits Baby Blanket (see New Arrivals). But try just drawing rather than appliqué so that you practise controlling the machine.

try outlining some simple motifs

Top tips for outlining

• Use a thread that contrasts well with the colour of your fabric.

• Try to keep the speed of the machine fairly constant and quite fast.

• Don't move the fabric too quickly – this will make the needle skip stitches.

• Remember you don't need to stop and move the hoop when you want to change direction. Keep your hoop facing the same way but just move it up or down or side to side to stitch the way you want to.

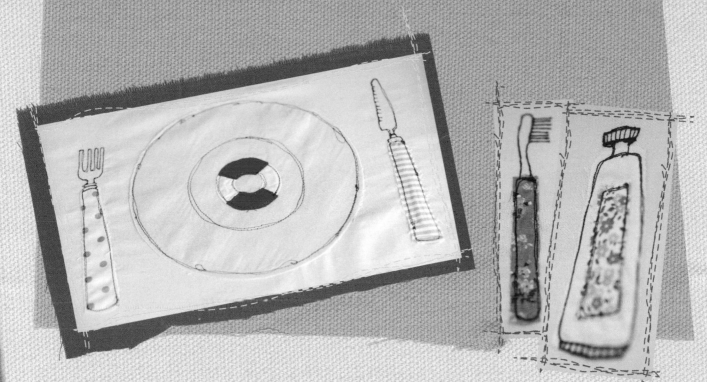

two Once you feel more confident, have a go at stitching some more complicated things – you could try drawing the knives and forks from the Tasty Teatime Tablecloth (see Party Time) or the toothbrush from the Happy Hols Wash Bag (see Happy Holidays). You will find that it is quite similar in some ways to drawing with a pencil – but quite different as well. You can take a pencil off the paper and move to another area; but with sewing, you have to stop the machine, remove the needle from the work and then move to your next area, trimming off the thread ends afterwards.

wall of inspiring images

three Once you get more confident, you'll find you can create some really nice effects by working from a drawing or photograph that you have in front of you. You could use a child's drawing, a favourite piece of art or just something cut out of a magazine. Place the image on the wall behind your sewing machine, so that you can see it when you look up, and try copying it. You will inevitably end up with a drawing that's more childlike and scribbly – but I think that's part of the charm of the technique. Keep things simple – and remember that wobbly lines are a thing of beauty in the world of freestyle sewing!

Shading

Shading is a really eye-catching way of filling an area of colour on a piece. It makes a nice alternative to appliqué, especially for smaller fiddly areas, and gives a more artistic, drawn look to your work. I love using shading on birds and animals as it give the impression of fur or feathers. It's also great for adding depth, giving a more three-dimensional quality to your work, and it also adds colour and detail. Here are four ways to use shading. Once you feel confident with the basics, experiment with different shapes, colours and types of stitches.

Basic shading

This technique is useful for filling in quite large areas with shading. It's simple, but very effective.

one Select your colours – one for the top thread and one for the bobbin. These could be the same colour, or you might want to try using two different ones.

tip : As with drawing, shading with the machine looks best if the stitches run in the same direction.

two Hoop up your fabric, place it under the needle and drop the foot. Lower the needle into the fabric and outline a roughly 2.5cm (1in) square.

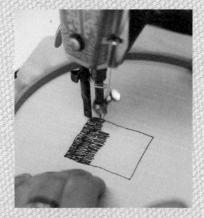

three Slowly start sewing within the square, moving the work back and forth by about 1cm (⅜in) to make a row of stitches across the fabric. Build up the shaded area, overlapping the rows slightly, until you have filled in your square.

Shading circles

Once you've mastered shading a square, have a go at shading a circle. Sew the outline of a circle roughly 2.5cm (1in) in diameter. Then move the work back and forth to fill in the circle with rows of stitching. Alternatively you could start in the centre and work outwards in circles to shade the area in – like drawing a spiral.

Using shading as part of a design

Once you feel confident, you can start to use shading as part of a design. Try outlining a motif (or you could do this in appliqué) and use shading to add colour and depth.

Use shading to add a touch of detail

You can use shading to fill in tiny areas of colour that are far too small to appliqué. I've used it on the Groovy Classes Case and the Oh-So-Bright Bookmark (see Happy Holidays). First make an outline in one colour then fill in with another colour, being careful to not go over your first line. You may need to get your fingers quite close to control the stitching as you are sewing something very small.

Top tips for shading

- Work back and forth in small areas.
- Exploit a mix of colour between your top thread and your bobbin thread.
- If the needle is bouncing a lot, tighten the tension.
- Make sure your hoop is really taut.
- Shading is trickier through lots of layers.

Appliqué

Appliqué is a lovely quick way to introduce colour to your work and you can layer up your appliqué pieces to create depth and intricacy. For example, I have created whole pieces just in detailed outlining and added a tiny bit of appliqué at the end for a dash of eye-catching colour. I've also made pieces such as a giant family portrait where I select a different fabric for every item of clothing and layer up the outfits and fit all the characters together – complicated and slow going but really satisfying once it's all stitched down!

Basic appliqué

To begin with it's best to stick to very simple exercises and easy fabrics. Try some simple shapes, a medium-weight cotton drill for the background fabric and brushed cotton for the appliqué.

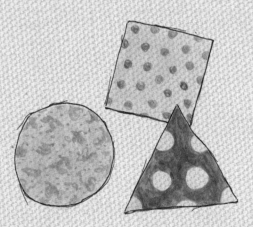

one Cut a selection of different shapes from your appliqué fabrics, making sure that your scissors are sharp and the edges do not fray too much.

two Place one of your shapes on your hooped-up background fabric and lower the needle into the top corner. Hold the appliqué piece in place with your fingertips so that your work keeps a lovely spontaneous look. However, if you really feel the urge to be neat and tidy, you could use a fine pin in the centre of the shape or fusible web to hold it in place.

three Slowly start to sew around the appliqué piece, moving the hoop while keeping the appliqué in place. Sew around the appliqué two or three times to make sure that it is really secure and can't fray too much. In general, sew a little way in from the edge – however, a wobbly line and a few scribbles can look very effective.

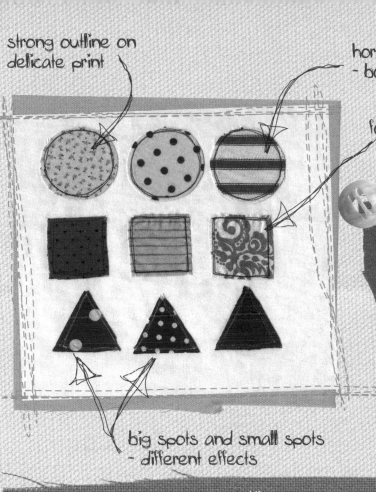

strong outline on
delicate print

horizontal stripes
- bold statement

focus on big ornate pattern

big spots and small spots
- different effects

Top tips for appliqué

- Pick fabric that won't fray too much.
- Pick a thread colour that contrasts nicely with your appliqué fabric.
- Avoid fabrics that have a coating or are too stretchy.
- Little patterns work really well.
- Exploit the pattern on your fabric as part of your design.

Appliqué troubleshooting

There are a couple of common problems with appliqué that I've developed various little tricks for solving:

- Often when you are stitching down a piece of appliqué, particularly a circle, it will look like it is going to pucker. If you catch it before it puckers too much you can stitch back over the line you have already sewn and approach the piece of fabric from the other direction. This often sorts the problem out. However if it's too late and you've got a bit of a pucker going on there are several things you can try. You could strategically add a little something to your design that goes over the puckered area, thus disguising it. You could use a bit of creative licence and scribble over the puckered area so it looks deliberate, and if you have a patterned fabric you could stitch around the pattern as if to accentuate the design, flattening out your pucker in the process.

- Another problem is mistakes, particularly spelling mistakes if you're writing or getting a face wrong if you're stitching a person. The best way to deal with these is to patch them over with a new piece of fabric and make it look like part of the design. Unpicking freehand embroidery can be really tricky and, I don't know about you, but I don't have the patience. So I just cut out a neat little patch and stitch it over the top of my mistake and no one is any the wiser!

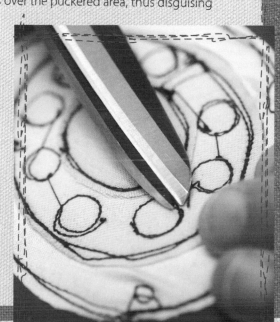

Shaped appliqué

Once you've mastered stitching the simple shapes, you can get started on some more complicated ones and begin to mix fabrics.

LOVE HEARTS

A heart is quite a simple shape to stitch – but it looks really sweet.

pretty scribbles

visible weave adds texture

multiple outlines

bobbin thread adds interest

stitching emphasizes heart shape

basic layering looks sweet

one Cut out a few hearts from different pink and red fabric scraps using the template supplied (see Templates).

two Sew the appliqué on with contrasting thread for a pretty effect.

tip: Try a little layering and grouping of different sized hearts. You could also experiment with bringing the bobbin thread through to the surface.

FUNKY FLOWERS

These flowers are a little trickier to cut out and stitch, but once you get used to them they are really simple and very effective.

one Cut each flower out of two contrasting fabrics using the template supplied (see Templates). Choose either a dark or pale fabric for the main flower and something contrasting for the centre spot.

two Lay the main flower onto your background fabric and then position the centre spot on top. You can stitch the flowers in two contrasting threads, using dark thread on light fabric and light thread on the dark.

tip: Have a play with layering and grouping different sized flowers to decide on the best arrangement before you stitch them down.

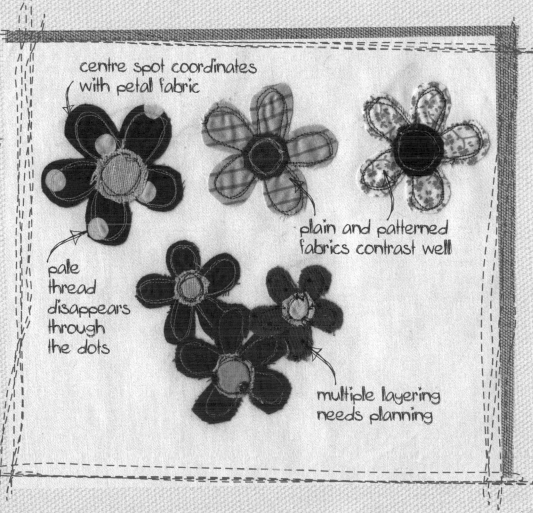

centre spot coordinates with petal fabric

plain and patterned fabrics contrast well

pale thread disappears through the dots

multiple layering needs planning

Layering appliqué

Layering allows you to use two or three different fabrics to build up your embroidery. I have used it here, combined with outlining and shading to stitch a butterfly but the technique is used throughout the projects in this book.

BUTTERFLY

This beautiful butterfly is simpler than it looks, but it does involve two different fabrics as well as outlining and shading. Select a plain fabric for one set of wings and a patterned fabric for the other.

one Cut out the shapes using the template supplied (see Templates).

two Lay the fabric for the bottom set of wings down first then lay the top set of wings so they overlap the bottom set just a little.

three First stitch the outline of the body and antennae of your butterfly, securing the pieces of the wings as you go. Then stitch round the wings in a thread that contrasts well with the fabric and add some lines to give definition to the wings.

four Finally use the shading technique to fill in the body of your butterfly. You could use a different colour again to add little dots to the end of its antennae.

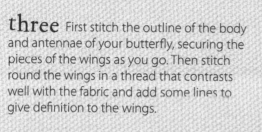

tip : You may want to pin your fabrics in position before you start, to stop them shifting and to ensure they overlap enough.

Developing your own creative appliqué

Making your own templates is a great way of making the freehand technique your own. Turn your favourite photo or image into a stitched masterpiece. Create something personal for friends or family and push the boundaries of drawing in stitches.

Once you have had a go at the other appliqué techniques and are starting to feel a little more comfortable with your machine, have a go at some of the projects. But sooner or later you're going to want to create something a little more unique and personal to you and that's where making your own templates comes in.

one Take a photo, a drawing you're pleased with, or an image you really like. It helps if the drawing has clear shapes and a good silhouette so you can see clearly how you can make it into appliqué. Some images, such as trees, lend themselves more to drawing with the machine while others, such as people, require a mix of appliqué and drawing.

two Make a drawing from your photo, either by tracing or freehand. Doing this freehand will help you to scale it up or down to how you need it. But you could also scale your drawing up or down on a photocopier. You need to accentuate the important lines in the object you're drawing and decide how the appliqué will be broken down into sections.

three Once you have decided which pieces you are going to appliqué and which parts you are going to embroider, trace your template from your original drawing, tracing off each element of the appliqué separately.

four Cut out your template and place on the relevant fabrics. Then draw round the templates and cut the fabrics out, just inside the line (or your could draw the design out on the reverse of the fabric so that your line wont show).

five Then it's business as usual, selecting the right colours to stitch down your lovely, unique, made-by-you design!

Finishing and edges

Raw edges are one of the unique aspects of the technique I use. They can be exploited to give extra texture and depth to the work or neatened with a bit of a haircut when you finish. I don't like my work to get too frayed and I like working with brushed cottons and closely woven cottons that give a nice neat edge. It's also amazing what a good old press will do to a piece of work – it's never completely finished until you've trimmed all your thread ends and pressed with plenty of steam!

a piece of selvedge edge adds some print to the piece

the raw edges emphasize the spikiness of the strawberry leaves

using felt means the handle and spout pieces on this teapot design won't fray

Ideas to try

- Use lighter weave fabric for smaller details such as flower petals so they don't fray away to nothing.
- Use looser weave fabrics where you want more texture, for example for trees and bushes around a house or in a garden.
- Use the torn edge of a fabric for fraying that is soft and uniform.
- Trim edges after you have appliquéd the fabric if they have become a bit too messy.
- Tease away weft threads after you have appliquéd the fabric to make a feature of the frayed edge.

tip : Practise with different types of fabric – from very closely woven winceyette (flannelette) to heavyweight furnishing fabrics – to get a feel for how each one behaves.

Finishing your embroidery

It may sound obvious but one of the key elements of producing a piece of work is finishing it off nicely. Once you've done your embroidery make sure you trim all your thread ends – though don't worry about the back if the project is lined. You don't need to worry about sewing ends in as your freehand stitching should be more than secure – though do make sure you do a little reverse stitch at the beginning and end of all your sewing.

Make sure you press your work on the reverse, using plenty of steam. Do this before you make a project up so you can really press the appliqué then give the whole project a quick press at the end, being careful not to burn or damage it. You may be in a rush to show off your new creation but remember... pressing makes perfect!

Troubleshooting

This technique has been known to drive some people completely round the bend – so it's not just you! It's tricky to give a complete troubleshooting guide when you'll all be working on different sewing machines but below are some of the most common problems you'll come across and the best way to tackle them.

Problem	Cause	Solution
NEEDLE SNAPPING	• Poor-quality needles • Tension too tight • Lack of practice	• Always buy the best quality needles – I find no.90 needles for wovens work best • Play with the tension to get it right – this will vary for all machines • Practise, practise, practise!
NEEDLE KEEPS SKIPPING STITCHES	• You may be moving your fabric and hoop too quickly	• Keep the hoop facing the same direction and move up and down and side to side rather than turning round while sewing – you can turn it round when you've stopped
THREAD BALLING UP IN THE BOBBIN CASE	• Foot not down on the machine • Tension wrong • Poor-quality thread • Ill-fitting bobbin • Build up of fluff in the machine	• Always make sure the foot lever is down, even if you're not using a foot • Play with the tension to get it right • Always use good-quality thread • Check the bobbin is in good order and fits the machine well • Keep the machine clean and well oiled
EMBROIDERY IS UNEVEN AND SKIPS STITCHES	• Machine incorrectly threaded • Needle wrong way round • Tension wrong • Unsuitable fabric • Poor-quality thread	• Check your manual to thread your machine and insert the needle correctly • Play with the tension to get it right • Try using a different fabric and see if things improve • Always use good-quality thread
HOOP LEAVES A STRONG CREASE ON THE FABRIC	• Hoop is too tight • Unsuitable fabric	• Ensure your hoop holds the fabric tightly without forcing the hoops together • Try different fabrics to see how they behave
STITCHING WON'T GET GOING ON A NEW PIECE OF APPLIQUÉ	• Appliqué piece is not held down and is bouncing away from the needle	• Hold the piece down with your fingers or the end of a little screwdriver • Allow the machine to stitch a couple of stitches on the spot before moving off
THREAD SNAPPING	• Poor-quality thread • Tension wrong • Build up of fluff in the machine • Machine incorrectly threaded • Thread caught round spool holder	• Always use good-quality thread • Play with the tension to get it right • Keep your machine clean and well oiled • Check your manual to thread your machine correctly • Gently tease out any thread that has got caught

Top tips for enjoying freehand machine embroidery

- Relax! Everything flows much better when you feel at one with the world and your sewing machine.

- Make sure you have a nice comfy chair and a good sewing position.

- Be inspired by your surroundings – make your workroom a place of sanctuary.

- Be inspired by your materials – treat yourself to some lovely fabrics that you can't wait to work with.

- Add personal touches, using a favourite old shirt that's worn out or a special button that means something to you.

- It's worth spending money on quality equipment. Cheap tools will just break or damage your work and make your life miserable!

- When everything goes wrong, take a break. Things usually look much better after coffee and cake.

- Get inspired by other artists. Do some research online, visit local galleries and craft shows and check out magazines like *Mollie Makes*, *Selvedge* and *Crafts*

- Keep things simple!

- Remember how clever you are and how impressed your friends will be when they see your handmade creations.

Projects

Now that you've spent many a happy hour stitching and scribbling without a care in the world it's time to get serious and actually make something! This is usually the point when your sewing machine breaks every five seconds, your needle snaps and you wonder why you didn't just stick to sewing the odd button on. But relax, enjoy and don't be too hard on yourself – with a little patience and plenty of practice you will make something fabulous!

Making up the projects

Once you've created a beautiful piece of embroidery, you'll want to use it on a project that looks equally professional. Follow the advice here to make sure you get the details just right. For the perfect finishing touch, you could add your signature or make a pretty label for your work.

Using the templates

Most of the templates you need for the projects appear at the back of the book in the Templates section, where you will also find plenty of ideas for motifs to appliqué. A lot of the projects give measurements for your fabric rather than templates. Some of the templates contain several elements and you will have to trace off each element separately. Some of the motifs use a lot of drawing as well as the template so a stitching guide is given in the Templates section.

one Select the relevant template from the Templates section at the back of the book. Identify how the template breaks down into separate appliqué pieces by looking at the photo of the finished item and trace off each element separately.

two Cut out the different elements of the template and select the different fabrics you are going to use to make up your motif. Place the templates upside down on the reverse side of your chosen fabrics and draw round them, keeping flush with the edge of the template.

three Cut out all the different elements of your motif and place them all together to make sure the design and fabric combination is working. With some designs you will be able to hoop up the whole motif in one go and in others you will need to place some of your appliqué pieces carefully to one side.

Seam allowances

A seam allowance of 1cm (⅜in) can be used on all the projects, and this has been allowed for on the project templates. Where the seam allowance differs from this, It Is specified in the project instructions. Of course, you don't need to think about seam allowances for the appliqué motifs!

Trimming seam corners

When you've got layers of fabric, the seams can be bulky, especially at the corners. The following technique will reduce that bulk quickly and simply, making projects look sharper.

After you have sewn your seam, cut across the corner at a 45-degree angle with a sharp pair of shears. Cut reasonably close to the stitching, but not so close that the fabric will fray at the corner when it is turned right side out.

tip : When you turn your work right side out, ensure that all the corners are fully pushed out. You can do this with your finger, the end of a chopstick or any other blunt point (such as the end of a paintbrush or similar) that you can wiggle into the corners.

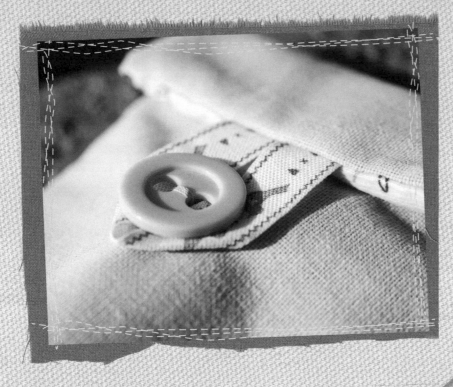

Making fabric loops

You can use pretty tape or ribbon to make button loops on your projects but loops made out of stitched fabric can be really useful and handy if you don't have any tape or ribbon. They're also great for hanging your projects and you can make them out of fabrics used in your project so everything goes nicely together.

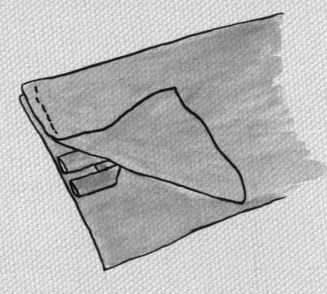

fold

one Cut a length of fabric about 5cm (2in) wide (you can adapt the width to suit the project or button). Fold the fabric in half lengthways and press.

two Open the fabric out, right side down, and fold each long edge over to meet along the original fold. Press the new folds.

three Fold the fabric along the original line again, encasing the long raw edges. Sew neatly along both long edges. The loop is then sewn into the inside of the seam as you construct the item.

tip : Make a much longer strip than you need and just cut off lengths for loops as and when you need them. It saves fiddling around with shorter lengths for individual loops.

Making handles

A good sturdy handle is essential for bags such as the Oh-So-Crafty Knitting Bag (see Getting Crafty) and the Beach Beautiful Backpack (see Happy Holidays). Use a fabric that is hardwearing, but not too bulky – the fabric is folded so many times it can easily get too thick to work with.

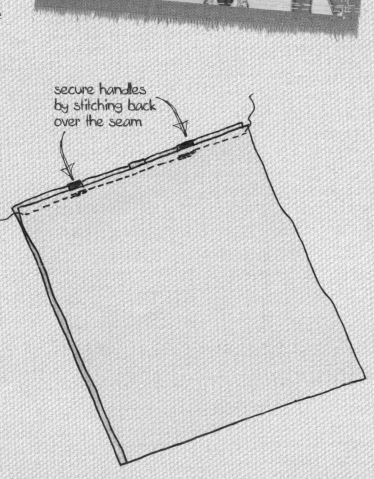

one Cut a strip of fabric for the handle. Measurements for the handles are given in the project steps but in general I like my handles to end up about 3cm (1⅛in) wide.

two Fold and press the ends of the strip to the wrong side. Then fold the strip lengthways to encase the long edges as described for fabric loops. Then stitch down the entire length of the handle as close to the edge as you can go.

secure handles by stitching back over the seam

three You don't need to worry about the ends of your handles as they will be sewn into the seam when you make up your project but make sure that when you stitch them in you go back over the seam to make sure it's really secure.

Personalizing your designs

Your designs will be very personal anyway, but you could add that extra special touch by adding a tiny motif on the back of your project or your signature. Using your sewing machine to sign your name might seem daunting, but practice makes perfect!

I sign everything I make and my signature was very wobbly at first – it's still pretty scribbly, but I think that's part of the charm. If you find writing too tricky, you could try adding a little motif such as a flower or smiley face.

Making a swing tag

Use good-quality cardboard and coloured ribbon to make a unique swing tag. You could design it on your computer or draw each one individually and photocopy them onto card. You can also buy very attractive plain gift tags, which you could customize.

Simple project ideas

If making up complicated projects is really not your cup of tea there are so many things you can do with your freehand embroidery skills.

- Even your little practice squares can become works of art in the right picture frame.
- Try the technique on something that is already made up – buy a plain apron or tea towel and stitch onto that.
- You could try using the technique to make a gorgeous badge or covered button (you can get great kids badge machines that will do the job or buy a simple button coverer from a sewing shop).
- Another really fun thing to do is to customize old clothes or household textiles. Instead of making up a tablecloth, for example, you could embroider your place settings onto a vintage tablecloth.

Really, once you get going with freehand machine embroidery, you will just want to scribble, stitch and appliqué onto anything you can get your hands on!

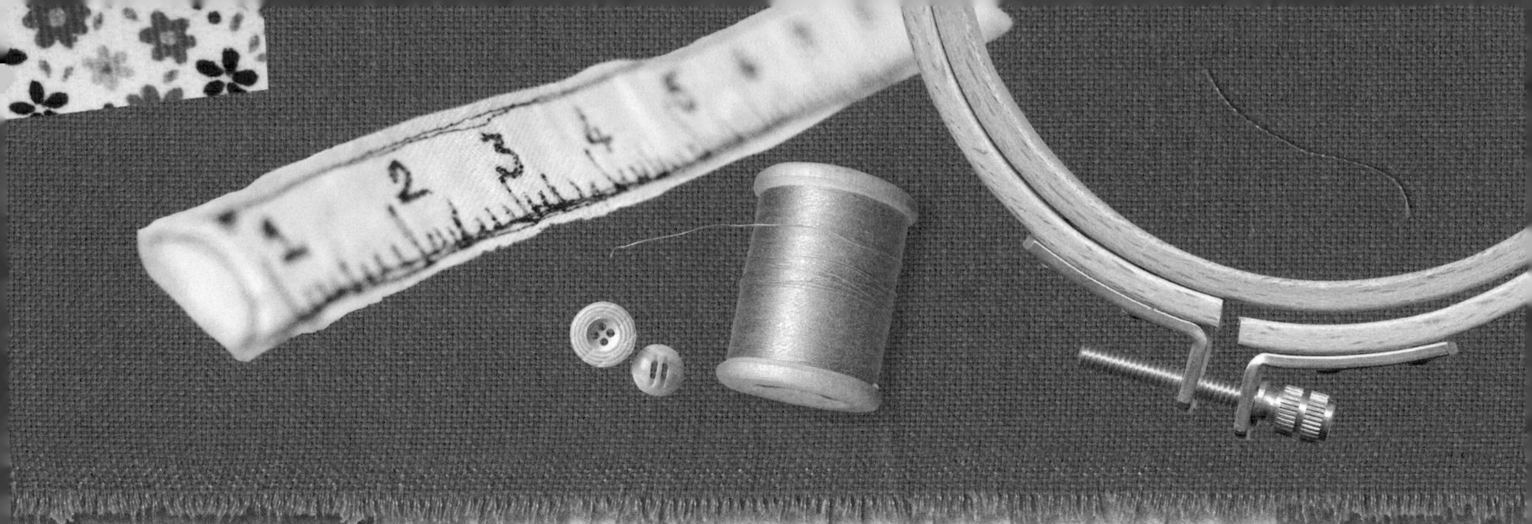

Getting Crafty

NIFTY NEEDLE CASE

PERKY POT PINCUSHION

SEW FABULOUS SEWING KIT

OH-SO-CRAFTY KNITTING BAG

NIFTY NEEDLE CASE

difficulty rating: **EASY PEASY**

You'll never need to hunt high and low for a needle again with this cute little needle case. It's simple to make but ever so useful and would make a great gift for a crafty friend.

pins and needles...all neat and tidy...

This little needle book was inspired by one I found in my grandma's old sewing box - hers was cross stitched but mine had to be freehand!

gather...

- 🍃 Templates (see Templates section)
- 🍃 1 piece of medium-weight base fabric, 13 x 18cm (5 x 7in)
- 🍃 2 pieces of lighter weight lining fabric, 13 x 9.5cm (5 x 3¾in)
- 🍃 1 piece of felt, 10 x 14cm (4 x 5½in)
- 🍃 Fabrics for the appliqué
- 🍃 10cm (4in) embroidery hoop

one Fold your base fabric piece in half and crease then crease the right-hand piece in half again. Make a small mark about halfway down your second crease – this is where your appliqué design will go.

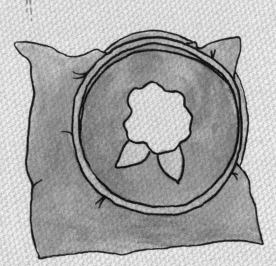

two Cut out your appliqué pieces using the templates. Hoop up and place your appliqué pieces over the dot you marked in step one. Embroider your design, trim and press.

tip : *Get a good effect for your rose motif by stitching with a scribbly sketchy style with more detail towards the centre of the flower.*

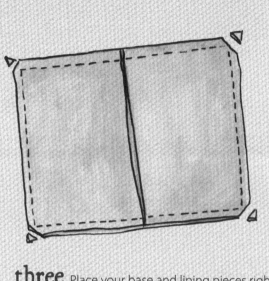

three Place your base and lining pieces right sides together and stitch round with a 1cm (⅜in) seam allowance. Leave the centre gap open then trim the corners off at an angle, turn through and press.

four Fold your piece of felt in half and crease. Place inside your needle case in line with your open seam so that an even amount of lining fabric shows on the other three sides.

tip: If you would like more pages in your case, use a thinner brushed cotton or winceyette (flannelette) instead of felt.

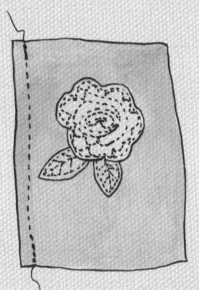

five Fold your case shut and sew down the spine around 5mm (³⁄₁₆in) from the edge, doing a little reverse stitch at the beginning and end to finish. Now go out and buy the prettiest pins and needles you can find – you deserve it!

PERKY POT PINCUSHION

difficulty rating: **EASY PEASY**

This dinky pincushion is the perfect reminder that you need to stop sewing and make a cup of tea very soon! It barely needs any fabric and will make use of any scrappy bits you were thinking of throwing out as you can use them for stuffing.

brewing up the perfect pincushion...

Earl Grey, milk, no sugar please (and a biscuit!)

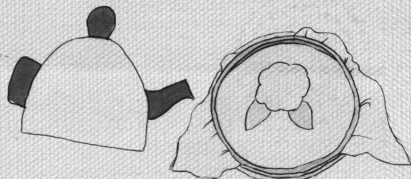

gather...

- ♡ Templates (see Templates section)
- ♡ 1 piece of base fabric, 25cm (10in) square (or you could use two or three smaller pieces)
- ♡ 1 piece of felt to cut out your handle, spout and knob
- ♡ Lots of fabric scraps, wadding or kapok for stuffing
- ♡ Fabrics for the appliqué
- ♡ 10cm (4in) embroidery hoop

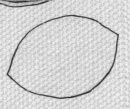

one Cut out all your pieces from the templates (the rose is the same as that used for the needle case in the previous project). Hoop up the front of your pincushion and embroider on your rose. Trim and press.

three Place the front and back pieces right sides together and insert your handle and spout pieces so that they are on the inside of your seam. Pin in place.

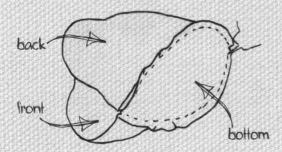

two Place your front piece and bottom piece right sides together and stitch around with a 5mm (³⁄₁₆in) seam allowance. Start and finish approximately 5mm (³⁄₁₆in) from the end of the front piece. Do the same with the back piece, matching the seams at the corners.

tip : Matching your seams up is quite tricky so have a practice with some scraps of fabric first.

four Leaving a 2.5cm (1in) gap at the top, stitch the front and back pieces together, turn through and stuff. For my stuffing I used fabric scraps chopped up really small.

five Fold in the edges of your opening, insert your little teapot knob in the centre of the seam and sew shut using a matching thread. You could do this on the machine or by hand. And, just like that, you're finished so go and put that kettle on!

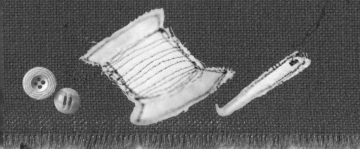

SEW FABULOUS SEWING KIT

difficulty rating: NOT TOO TRICKY

This cosy pouch will keep all you sewing essentials neatly in one place whether you're on the move or just need a place for everything. It's a little trickier to make but take it steady and remember you'll have somewhere to put all your lovely sewing bits and bobs when you finish!

sew organized...and scrummy too!

This sewing pouch has space for all your sewing essentials and a special section for a sketchbook – perfect for storing all that inspiration!

gather...

- ♡ Templates (see Templates section)
- ♡ 1 piece of fairly stiff base fabric (such as coloured canvas or denim), 26 x 48cm (10¼ x 19in)
- ♡ 1 piece of lighter-weight lining fabric, 26 x 48cm (10¼ x 19in)
- ♡ 1 piece of the same lining fabric, 12 x 30cm (4¾ x 12in) for the pocket
- ♡ 1 piece of wadding (batting), 26 x 48cm (10¼ x 19in)
- ♡ 1cm (⅜in) wide elastic, 36cm (14in) long
- ♡ Pretty ribbon or webbing, 80cm (30in) long
- ♡ 20cm (8in) embroidery hoop

tuck wadding (batting) into fold

one Cut out your appliqué pieces using the templates. Lay out on your base fabric to get the spacing right. Place the pieces to one side then hoop up one piece at a time and stitch on, moving the hoop for each piece. Trim and press then place to one side.

two Take your lining and wadding (batting) pieces. Fold over approximately 1.5cm (½in) of the right-hand side of your lining piece. Place the wadding (batting) with the lining piece, wrong sides together and tuck the end of the wadding (batting) into the fold.

tip : Sometimes your fabric may not completely fill the hoop as this design comes quite close to the edge of the fabric. Just make sure it's pulled nice and taut. Alternatively start with a larger piece of fabric and trim it down afterwards.

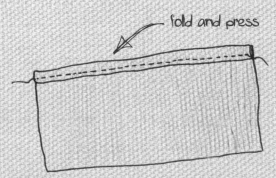

fold and press

three Take the pocket piece, fold and press the top edge over by 1cm (⅜in). Repeat and stitch the fold down.

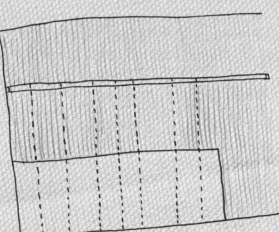

four Fold and press the right-hand side of your pocket piece over by 1cm (⅜in). Repeat and place on to the left-hand bottom edge of the lining piece and wadding, keeping the folded end of the lining to the right. Pin in place then stitch the pocket down, leaving the top edge open.

tip : I used ticking fabric for the lining to help me mark out my intervals and sew in a straight line!

five Place your elastic approximately 10cm (4in) down from the top of the lining piece in line with the left-hand side. Stitch down at both ends then stitch down at intervals carrying your seam on to sew dividers in the pocket. These will be the slots for your various utensils, bits and bobs.

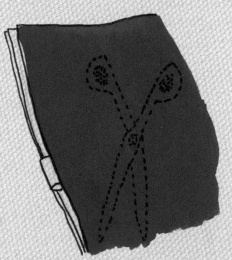

six Now place your embroidered base piece and lining/wadding (batting) sandwich right sides together and iron over 1.5cm (½in) on the right-hand side of your embroidered piece so that it's the same length as the lining piece. Fold your ribbon or webbing in half, insert it inside the left-hand seam about halfway down and pin in place.

seven Stitch round the whole thing with a 1.5cm (½in) seam allowance leaving the right-hand folded edges open. Trim your corners, turn through and press.

eight Sew the folded edge shut. Fold this end over so that it lines up with the right-hand edge of your pocket and stitch down the top and bottom edges, sewing about 2mm (¹⁄₁₆in) from the edge. If this is too bulky for your machine, you will need to hand sew this part.

nine Insert your precious haberdashery into the slots (a notebook in the pocket helps make everything nice and stiff), tie the ribbon around the case and get yourself down to your nearest sewing group for some serious showing off!

OH-SO-CRAFTY KNITTING BAG

difficulty rating: **A BIT MORE TRICKY**

When I'm not sewing, I'm knitting, so I designed this bag with knitting needs in mind. It's pretty big to fit in all those yummy yarns, there's a divided pocket for needles and patterns, it has a little felt needle book built in, and the whole thing ties shut with soft webbing ties ... perfect!

nifty knitting...out and about...

This bag has a handy divided pocket for storing your needles, patterns and knitting accessories. There's also plenty of room for your yarn and even a good book!

gather...

♡ Templates (see Templates section)

♡ 2 pieces of base fabric, 50cm (20in) square

♡ 1 piece of base fabric, 25 x 50cm (10 x 20in), for the pocket

♡ 2 pieces of lining fabric, 50cm (20in) square

♡ 1 piece of lining fabric, 25 x 50cm (10 x 20in), for the pocket

♡ 2 pieces of backed wadding (batting), 50cm (20in) square

♡ 2 pieces of handle fabric, 62 x 10cm (24½ x 4in)

♡ 2.5cm (1in) wide natural herringbone webbing, 20cm (8in) long

♡ 1 small piece of felt

♡ Fabrics for the appliqué

♡ 20cm (8in) embroidery hoop

one Use the templates to cut out your appliqué pieces. Lay them out on your base fabric so you're happy with the composition, making small positioning marks underneath the pieces if necessary. Use chalk or a ballpoint pen to mark a start and finish point for the washing line, approximately 9cm (3½in) from the top.

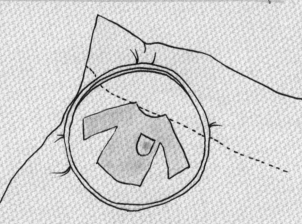

two Use a straight running stitch and dark contrasting thread and bobbin to stitch the washing line. Hoop up your fabric, set your machine back to freehand and stitch on your appliqué pieces one by one, moving the hoop each time and placing your other pieces carefully to one side. Once you've sewn all the motifs, trim all your thread ends and press.

tip : If you rip your strips of fabric you'll actually get a much straighter line than trying to cut them.

three Prepare your bag handles (see Making handles in the Making up the projects section). Prepare your pocket by placing the two 25cm (10in) fabric pieces right sides together. Fold up the bottom long edge of the front piece by 1.5cm (½in) and press. Turn the whole pocket over and do the same on the other side. Stitch all around with a 1.5cm (½in) seam allowance from the bottom right to the bottom left leaving the bottom folded edge open.

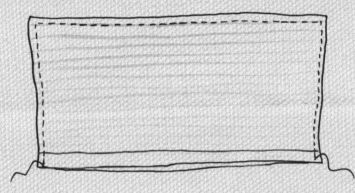

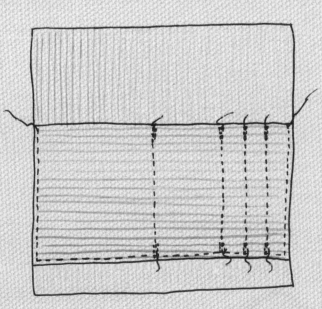

four Trim the corners and turn the pocket through and press. Use the iron to fold and press the pocket to mark your stitching lines for the dividers. Fold the whole pocket in half and press to crease, unfold then fold the right-hand half in half, press and unfold. Finally fold the right-hand quarter into thirds and press. When you unfold it you should have four dividing lines.

five Place your pocket onto one of your lining pieces approximately 18cm (7in) from the top and pin in place. Then, starting from the top right of the pocket, stitch it onto the lining, sewing as close to the edge as you can, making sure you do a reverse stitch at the beginning and end to secure it. Then stitch your dividing lines again using a reverse stitch at the beginning and end to secure.

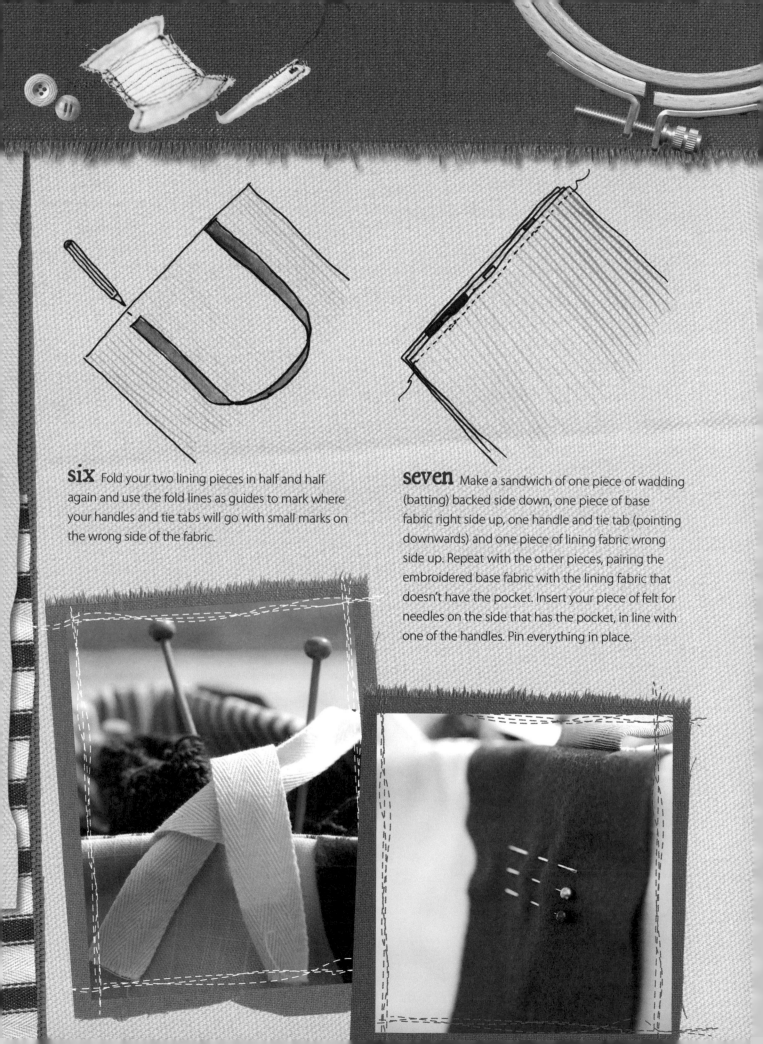

six Fold your two lining pieces in half and half again and use the fold lines as guides to mark where your handles and tie tabs will go with small marks on the wrong side of the fabric.

seven Make a sandwich of one piece of wadding (batting) backed side down, one piece of base fabric right side up, one handle and tie tab (pointing downwards) and one piece of lining fabric wrong side up. Repeat with the other pieces, pairing the embroidered base fabric with the lining fabric that doesn't have the pocket. Insert your piece of felt for needles on the side that has the pocket, in line with one of the handles. Pin everything in place.

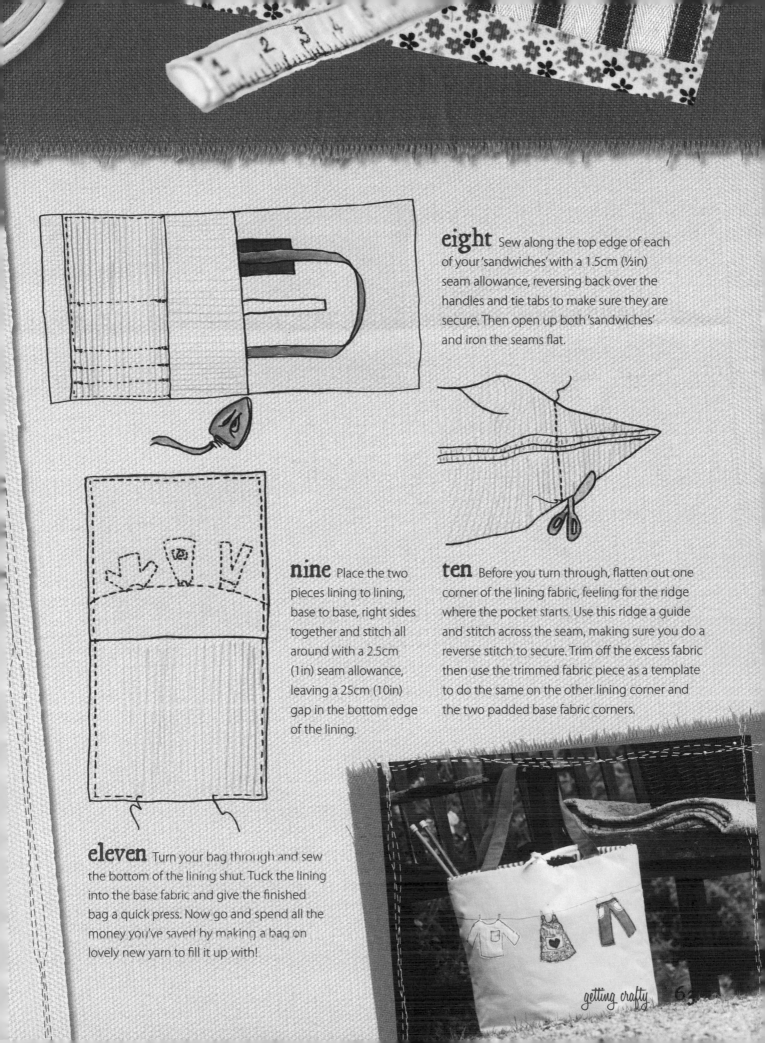

eight Sew along the top edge of each of your 'sandwiches' with a 1.5cm (½in) seam allowance, reversing back over the handles and tie tabs to make sure they are secure. Then open up both 'sandwiches' and iron the seams flat.

nine Place the two pieces lining to lining, base to base, right sides together and stitch all around with a 2.5cm (1in) seam allowance, leaving a 25cm (10in) gap in the bottom edge of the lining.

ten Before you turn through, flatten out one corner of the lining fabric, feeling for the ridge where the pocket starts. Use this ridge a guide and stitch across the seam, making sure you do a reverse stitch to secure. Trim off the excess fabric then use the trimmed fabric piece as a template to do the same on the other lining corner and the two padded base fabric corners.

eleven Turn your bag through and sew the bottom of the lining shut. Tuck the lining into the base fabric and give the finished bag a quick press. Now go and spend all the money you've saved by making a bag on lovely new yarn to fill it up with!

New Arrivals

TOOTH FAIRY PILLOW POUCH

BONNY BABY BIB

NURSERY TOYS WALL ART

SUMMER FRUITS BABY BLANKET

TOOTH FAIRY PILLOW POUCH

difficulty rating: **EASY PEASY**

This cute pouch is very simple to make and involves just a little bit of sewing magic. It makes a perfect new baby gift and is a lovely keepsake when the little ones are all grown up. You could choose different colours to make it more suitable for a boy.

tooth fairy please call tonight...

Use a silky lining to make this little purse extra special.

gather...

♡ Templates (see Templates section)

♡ 1 piece of medium- to heavyweight base fabric, 30 x 12cm (12 x 4¾in)

♡ 1 piece of medium- to lightweight fabric for the lining, 30 x 12cm (12 x 4¾in)

♡ Fabrics for the appliqué

♡ 10cm (4in) embroidery hoop

tip : To get the face to look cute, make the eyes big by moving your hoop in tiny circles. Sew only one line for the mouth with a tiny reverse stitch at the beginning and end to secure it.

one Fold your base fabric piece into thirds and press, then open out so you have two clear creases, these will be the guide for where to put your appliqué. Mark the ends of the creases with two small pen marks on the reverse side.

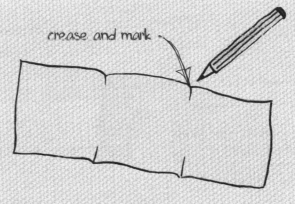

crease and mark

two Cut out your appliqué pieces using the templates. Hoop up the end third of your base fabric with the excess fabric towards the top and stitch your appliqué so that the feet of your fairy face the end of your fabric.

three Place your base fabric and lining right sides together and stitch round the end section (the one with your appliqué on it) with a 5mm (3/16in) seam allowance, starting and finishing at your crease marks.

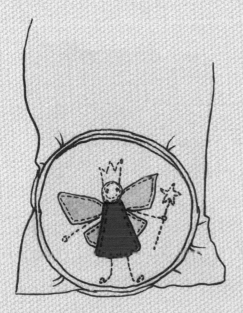

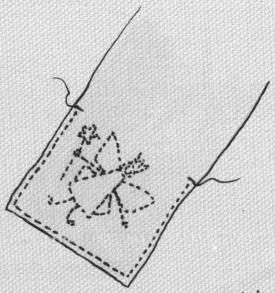

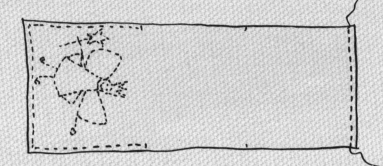

four Sew the other end of your base and lining fabric together with the same seam allowance and trim the corners at an angle – at this point this little bag seems like it's not going to work but trust me – it all comes together in the end!

five Open out your fabric so that your seam from step four lines up with your seam from step three, linings together and base fabrics together, and press. Cut open the lining fabric along the new crease – don't worry I know what I'm doing!

crease and cut

six Stitch the sides of the lining pieces together with a 5mm (³/₁₆in) seam allowance ending at the point where the previous seams meet. Do the same with the sides of the base fabric pieces. Trim your corners and turn through.

seven Fold in the final seam and sew shut, tuck the lining into the bag, press and you're done. Now tell the kids to get wobbling those teeth!

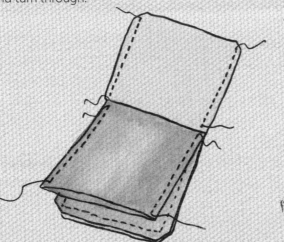

fold in and stitch down

BONNY BABY BIB

difficulty rating: **EASY PEASY**

This jolly little bib is perfect for boys and girls and great for special occasions or just as an accessory to a pretty outfit. You could make it with the apple motif given here or use other motifs that you find throughout the book.

you are the apple of my eye...

gather...

♡ Templates (see Templates section)

♡ 1 piece of medium- to lightweight base fabric, at least 21cm (8¼in) square

♡ 1 piece of lightweight fabric for the lining, at least 21cm (8¼in) square

♡ 2 pieces of ribbon for the ties, 25cm (10in) long

♡ Fabrics for the appliqué

♡ 10cm (4in) embroidery hoop

one Cut out the base, lining and appliqué pieces using the templates. Hoop up your base piece and stitch on your appliqué, using a dark navy or black thread. Trim and press.

two Place your base and lining pieces right sides together and stitch round with 5mm (³⁄₁₆in) seam allowance starting at the right side of the neck. Insert the ends of your ribbons on the inside of the seam at the tips of the bib neck as you go and leave around an 8cm (3in) gap in the neck for turning through.

three Turn through, fold in the final seam and press the whole thing. Then stitch all the way round your bib, closing the final seam as you go. Stitch around 2mm (¹⁄₁₆in) from the edge and use either a matching thread or something that deliberately contrasts to add a nice border. Now stop sewing and go mash some banana!

insert ribbon

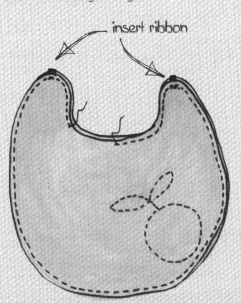

tip : It might be a good idea to wash the fabrics you are going to use first to make sure they're dribble proof! This will also prevent any shrinking during future washes.

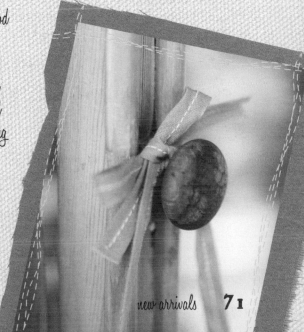

NURSERY TOYS WALL ART

difficulty rating: **NOT TOO TRICKY**

This brightly coloured patchwork-style design will look great in any child's bedroom. You could match the colours to curtains, walls and rugs or go crazy and multicoloured like I have. Either way you'll have fun making it!

my bestest ever toys...

This stitched picture will add that extra sparkle to the nursery wall.

gather...

- ♡ Templates (see Templates section)
- ♡ 1 piece of medium-weight base fabric, 40 x 50cm (15¾ x 20in) (you could scale this up or down to fit a specific frame if you have one already)
- ♡ 9 pieces of lightweight fabric, 17 x 14cm (6½ x 5½in)
- ♡ Fabrics for the appliqué
- ♡ 20cm (8in) embroidery hoop
- ♡ A frame, mount and strong fabric tape/gaffer tape (or take it to be framed once it's done!)

one Cut out your appliqué pieces using the templates. Please read the advice in the Making up the projects section on how to use the templates as they can be quite tricky! Spend a little time laying out your squares and appliqué bits to make sure you're happy with the colour combinations

two Once you have your squares how you want them, place your appliqué pieces to one side and gather up one row of squares at a time. Stitch the squares together down the longest side with a 1cm (⅜in) seam allowance. Press on the reverse, opening up the seams and pressing flat.

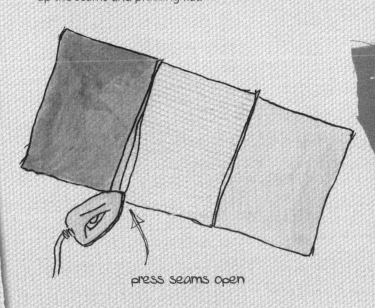

press seams open

three Sew the three rows together, again with a 1cm (⅜in) seam allowance and making sure the seams line up as best as they can – though a little quirky wonkiness is always fine! Press your seams flat.

four Working on the reverse, fold in the side edges by 1cm (⅜in). Press the folds and trim the corners then fold in the top and bottom edges by 1cm (⅜in) and press.

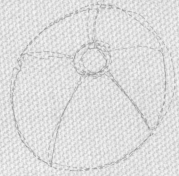

five Sew your squares onto your base fabric using a contrasting thread and stitching around 3mm (⅛in) from the edge. This stitching will form a border around your wall art.

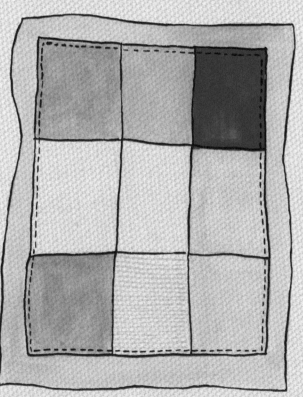

six Hoop up with the 20cm (8in) hoop and stitch your motifs on one by one, always making sure you are choosing your thread colour so that it really contrasts with your appliqué fabric and your stitching stands out.

tip: Personalize your wall art by adding a name or a favourite toy. See Developing your own creative appliqué in the Techniques section to help you with this.

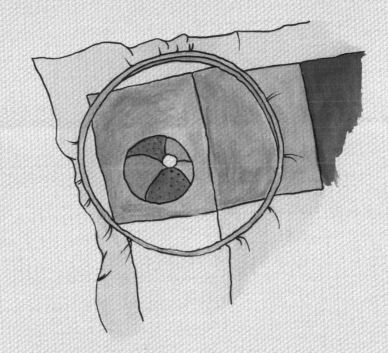

seven Press the whole piece on the reverse and place onto your backing board (if you are framing it yourself). Stick down with strong fabric tape (such as gaffer tape) making sure the tape won't show under your mount. Place your board and mount inside your frame. Now find a big strong man to put a nail in the wall so you can hang it up!

SUMMER FRUITS BABY BLANKET

difficulty rating: **A BIT MORE TRICKY**

This gorgeous little quilt is the perfect gift for that new addition to the family. It's really eye catching and looks a lot trickier than it actually is. You could customize the design using your own special fabrics or changing the colours to be more boyish. Either way it's well worth the effort!

This small blanket is a great introduction to quilting with freehand embroidery.

snug as a bug in a rug...

gather...

- ♡ Templates (see Templates section)
- ♡ 9 pieces of medium-weight fabric, 27cm (10½in) square (I used 4 patterned and 5 plain ones)
- ♡ 1 piece of medium-weight fabric for the backing, 75cm (29½in) square
- ♡ 1 piece of wadding (batting), 75 x 74cm (29½ x 29in)
- ♡ Fabrics for the appliqué
- ♡ 20cm (8in) or 25cm (10in) embroidery hoop
- ♡ A nice big clear surface (I know it's a tall order!)
- ♡ Ribbon to tie it up as a gift (optional)

one Lay out your squares to decide your composition then cut out your appliqué pieces using the templates and lay out on your squares. I put my appliqué on the plain squares and left the patterned ones blank, but feel free to mix it up!

two Stack your squares carefully so that the appliqué pieces don't blow away, then hoop up your squares one by one. You will need to place some of the pieces that don't fit into the hoop carefully to one side (don't lose them!) – you can then move your hoop to complete each square. Remove from the hoop and trim then press.

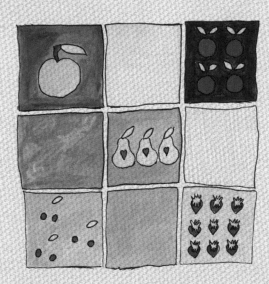

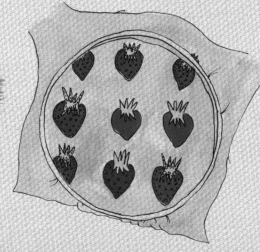

tip: Use masculine colours; blues, creams and greens for a boy or neutral colours such as beiges, sage greens and browns for a surprise baby. The fruit design will work well with either of these colour schemes.

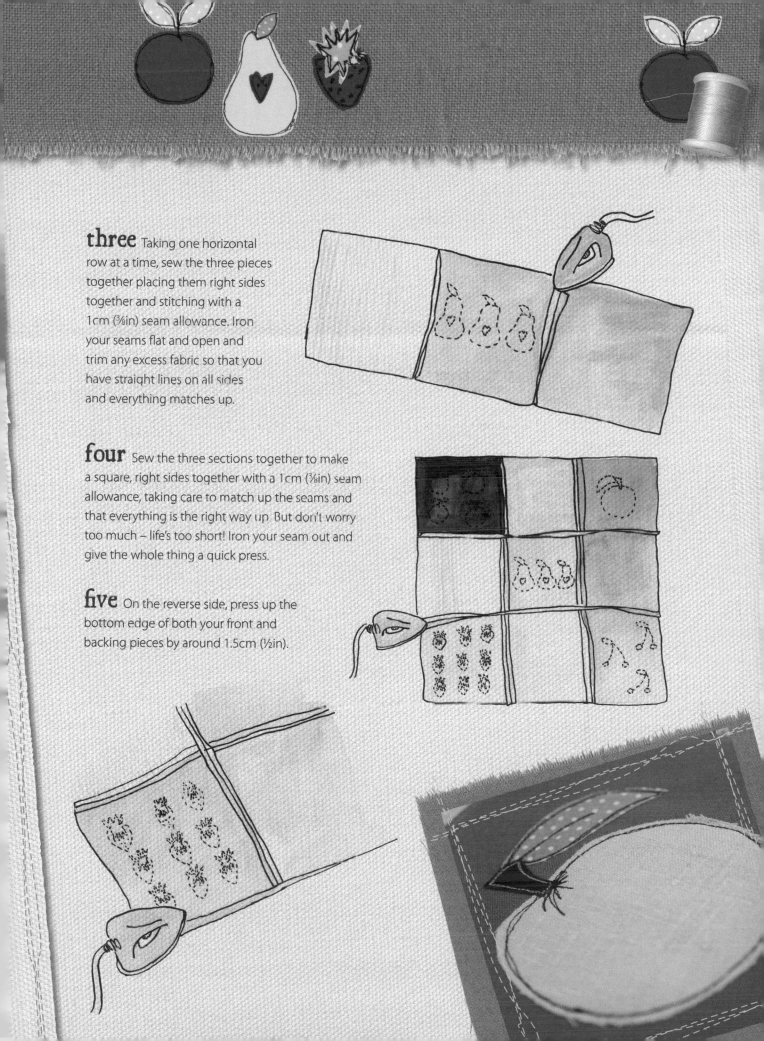

three Taking one horizontal row at a time, sew the three pieces together placing them right sides together and stitching with a 1cm (⅜in) seam allowance. Iron your seams flat and open and trim any excess fabric so that you have straight lines on all sides and everything matches up.

four Sew the three sections together to make a square, right sides together with a 1cm (⅜in) seam allowance, taking care to match up the seams and that everything is the right way up. But don't worry too much – life's too short! Iron your seam out and give the whole thing a quick press.

five On the reverse side, press up the bottom edge of both your front and backing pieces by around 1.5cm (½in).

six Place the front and backing pieces right sides together, tuck your wadding (batting) into the fold on one side and pin. Stitch all the way round with a 1.5cm (½in) seam allowance leaving your folded edge open and checking carefully that all pieces of the 'sandwich' are caught.

seven Trim round the whole thing to neaten the edges and prevent them becoming too bulky, but leave at least 1cm (⅜in) of fabric. Trim your corners at an angle. Remove the pins, turn through and press.

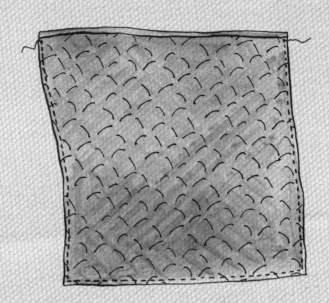

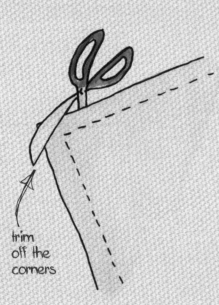

trim off the corners

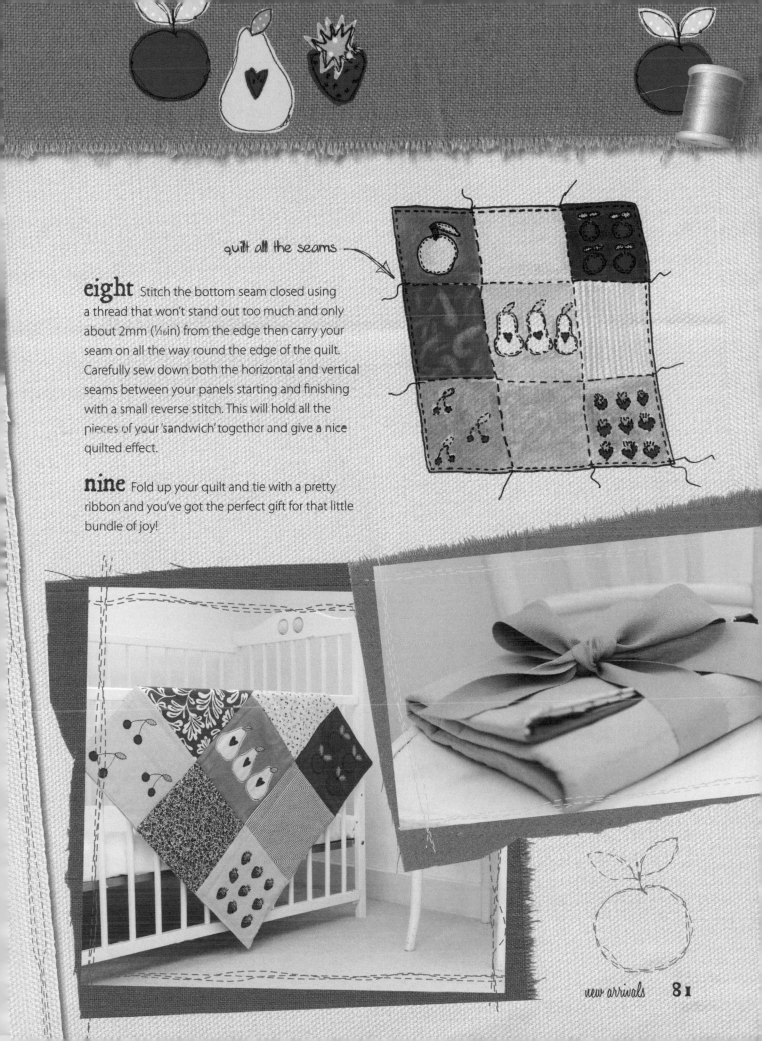

quilt all the seams

eight Stitch the bottom seam closed using a thread that won't stand out too much and only about 2mm (¹⁄₁₆in) from the edge then carry your seam on all the way round the edge of the quilt. Carefully sew down both the horizontal and vertical seams between your panels starting and finishing with a small reverse stitch. This will hold all the pieces of your 'sandwich' together and give a nice quilted effect.

nine Fold up your quilt and tie with a pretty ribbon and you've got the perfect gift for that little bundle of joy!

Party Time

BEACHY BOATY BUNTING

NATTY NAME TAGS

SUPER-SPECIAL PARTY BAG

TASTY TEATIME TABLECLOTH

BEACHY BOATY BUNTING

difficulty rating: **EASY PEASY**

Follow these simple steps to produce the smartest bunting in town (or country). It's the sort of bunting that will be treasured for a lifetime and brought out for every celebration, be it a family wedding or a Sunday roast!

bunting blowing in the breeze...

Red, white and blue are the perfect colours for a nautical feel.

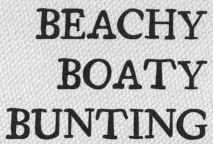

gather...

♡ Templates (see Templates section)

♡ 13 pieces of medium-weight fabric at least 15 x 20cm (6 x 8in) (you choose your colours, I went nautical with cream, blue and red but anything goes!)

♡ Fabric for the backs of the triangles, approximately 0.5m (½yd)

♡ 2.5cm (1in) wide cotton webbing, 3m (3¼yd) long

♡ Chopstick or other such pointy tool

♡ Fabrics for the appliqué

♡ 10cm (4in) embroidery hoop

one Use the triangle template to cut your bunting pieces, mixing the fabrics up for the front pieces and using your plain fabric for the backs of the triangles. Then use the smaller templates to cut out your appliqué pieces.

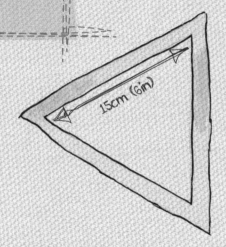

15cm (6in)

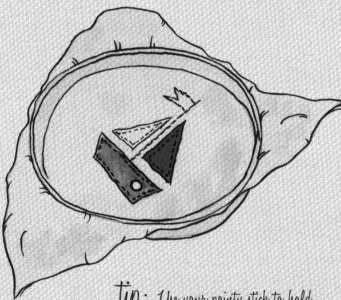

two Hoop up your triangles and carefully stitch on your appliqué pieces. Don't forget to add a little flag at the top of the boat and a porthole in white. You can appliqué every triangle or every other one – it's up to you and your patience! Once stitched, trim off all your thread ends and press.

tip : Use your pointy stick to hold down the tiny pieces of appliqué as you stitch them – so your fingers don't have to go quite so far into the danger zone!

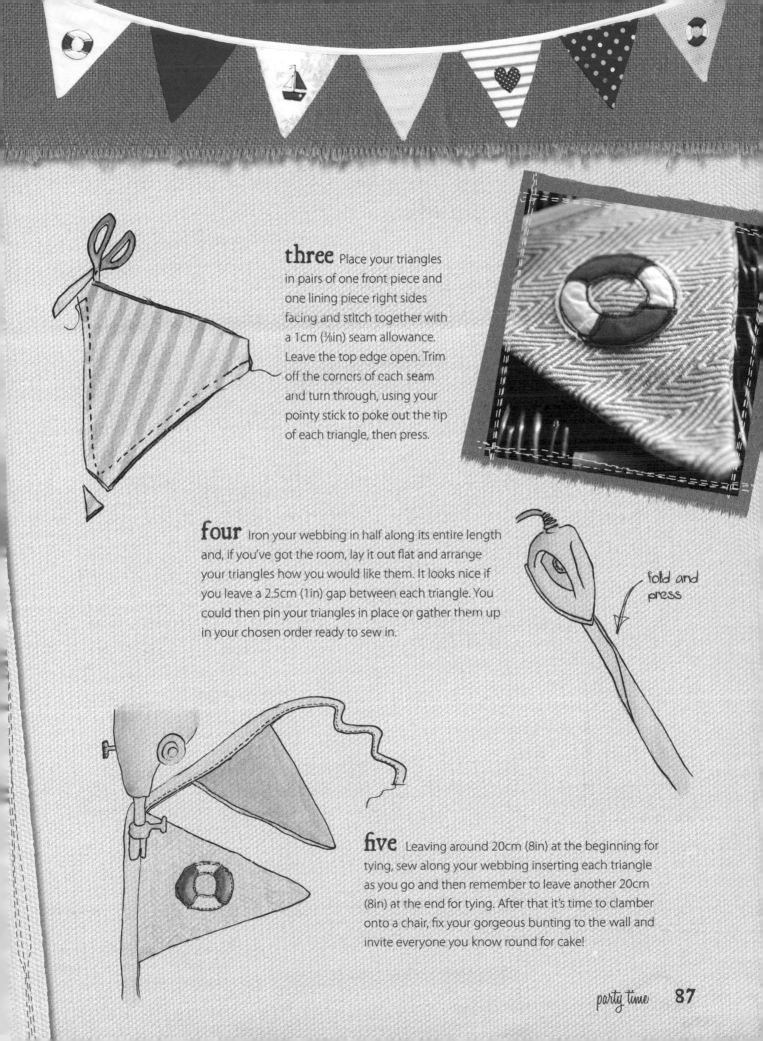

three Place your triangles in pairs of one front piece and one lining piece right sides facing and stitch together with a 1cm (⅜in) seam allowance. Leave the top edge open. Trim off the corners of each seam and turn through, using your pointy stick to poke out the tip of each triangle, then press.

four Iron your webbing in half along its entire length and, if you've got the room, lay it out flat and arrange your triangles how you would like them. It looks nice if you leave a 2.5cm (1in) gap between each triangle. You could then pin your triangles in place or gather them up in your chosen order ready to sew in.

fold and press

five Leaving around 20cm (8in) at the beginning for tying, sew along your webbing inserting each triangle as you go and then remember to leave another 20cm (8in) at the end for tying. After that it's time to clamber onto a chair, fix your gorgeous bunting to the wall and invite everyone you know round for cake!

NATTY NAME TAGS

difficulty rating: **EASY PEASY**

These terrific tags will make the perfect finishing touch to the table on that special occasion – or you could just make one for yourself! The writing will take a little practice and if you chicken out you could always write it on with washable pen (but don't tell any one I said so!)

gather...

- ♡ Templates (see Templates section)
- ♡ 1 piece of medium-weight base fabric, 14 x 20cm (5½ x 8in) for each tag
- ♡ 1 piece of medium-weight lining fabric, 14 x 20cm (5½ x 8in) for each tag
- ♡ 1 piece of ribbon, 30cm (12in) long for each tag
- ♡ Fabrics for the appliqué
- ♡ 10cm (4in) embroidery hoop
- ♡ Chopstick or other such pointy tool

draw but don't cut

one Take your base fabric and draw around the tag template but don't cut it out just yet as it will be too small for your hoop. Cut out your appliqué pieces using the templates and lay them out on the base fabric to see how it's looking.

two Leaving your bunting triangles to one side, hoop up and stitch on your name panel, stitching around the outside two or three times then stitching on your name. Remove from the hoop, trim and press.

three Now you can cut out your base and lining fabrics as per the template. Once you've done that press up about 5mm (³⁄₁₆in) on the wide end of each piece, working on the reverse.

four Lay out your base fabric right side up and line up your bunting triangles along the top edge – they may overlap slightly but that's fine. Fold your ribbon in half and place it at the thin end so that it will be on the inside of the seam.

tip : Practise the writing first on a scrap of similar weight fabric. Stitch each name you want to use at least five times and they should start to look pretty good!

five Place your lining fabric face down on top of all the other bits and pin if necessary. Stitch round with a 5mm (³⁄₁₆in) seam allowance leaving the folded edge open. Trim the corners and turn through, using a chopstick or other pointy tool if necessary to get everything nice and crisp. Then press.

six Sew your end seam shut using a matching thread then continue to stitch round about 2mm (¹⁄₁₆in) from the edge to give a decorative edge to your tag, sewing a little reverse stitch at the start and finish. Now if you're anything like me you'll pour yourself a large glass of red, tie your tag round it and sit back and enjoy – those guests can wait!

the finishing touch to your party table...

SUPER-SPECIAL PARTY BAG

difficulty rating: **NOT TOO TRICKY**

This gorgeous bag is definitely a step above the average party bag but it's really not too tricky to make. Your guests will be so very impressed and who knows what you'll get in return next time they throw a party!

a parting gift to sail away with...

Bunting and boats make this a perfect party bag for a seasidey shindig.

gather...

♡ Templates (see Templates section)

♡ 2 pieces of base fabric, 30 x 26cm (12 x 10¼in) (I used a stiff canvas-type fabric that worked very well)

♡ 2 pieces of 2.5cm (1in) wide webbing for handles, 40cm (15 ¾in) long

♡ Fabrics for the appliqué

♡ 20cm (8in) embroidery hoop

tip: *As this is meant to be a quick project that you can make for a number of guests, it's not lined but you could always stitch in a lining to make it into more of an everyday bag.*

tuck handle into fold

one Cut out your appliqué pieces using the templates. Hoop up and stitch on the boat appliqué, placing it towards the bottom of one of your base pieces. Remove from the hoop, trim and press.

tip: *Make sure you trim your threads nicely on this one as this little bag isn't lined so the reverse of your embroidery will show.*

two With the right side up, fold over the top edge of your fabric by 1.5cm (½in) and tuck both ends of your webbing in, approximately 6cm (2½in) from each side.

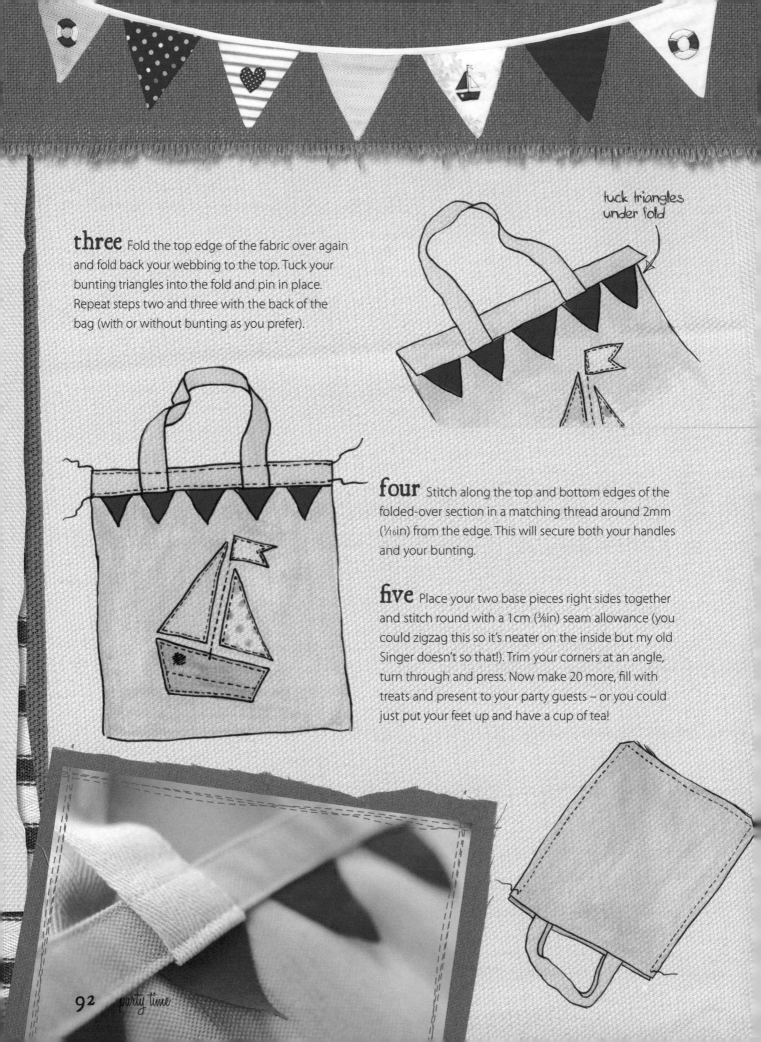

tuck triangles
under fold

three Fold the top edge of the fabric over again and fold back your webbing to the top. Tuck your bunting triangles into the fold and pin in place. Repeat steps two and three with the back of the bag (with or without bunting as you prefer).

four Stitch along the top and bottom edges of the folded-over section in a matching thread around 2mm (1/16in) from the edge. This will secure both your handles and your bunting.

five Place your two base pieces right sides together and stitch round with a 1cm (3/8in) seam allowance (you could zigzag this so it's neater on the inside but my old Singer doesn't so that!). Trim your corners at an angle, turn through and press. Now make 20 more, fill with treats and present to your party guests – or you could just put your feet up and have a cup of tea!

TASTY TEATIME TABLECLOTH

difficulty rating: **A BIT MORE TRICKY**

This wonderfully eye-catching tablecloth will make any tea party go with a swing. The pattern here is for a square cloth that would also work for a round table but you could easily adapt it for a rectangular table.

the prettiest table in town...

Set off your homemade cakes with a handmade tablecloth.

gather...

- ♡ Templates (see Templates section)
- ♡ 1 piece of lightweight plain fabric, 1.5m (1½yd) (I used bright white curtain lining)
- ♡ Fabrics for the appliqué (I used ivory curtain lining for my plates)
- ♡ 20cm (8in) embroidery hoop
- ♡ A nice big clear surface (preferably the table you are making the cloth for!)

one Measure the width of your fabric, selvedge to selvedge, and cut so that the length is the same as the width plus around 2cm (¾in) on each end for hemming. Fold in the cut edges by 1cm (⅜in), repeat, press and stitch down with a matching thread.

two Fold your tablecloth into quarters then in half and press. You can use these creases to help place your appliqué. Make a small mark where each place setting will go halfway along each side and around halfway between the edge and middle.

tip: If you have a smaller, larger or rectangular table then you can make your fabric longer or sew two pieces together and mark your place settings out by laying the cloth on the table and making small marks for each one.

creases

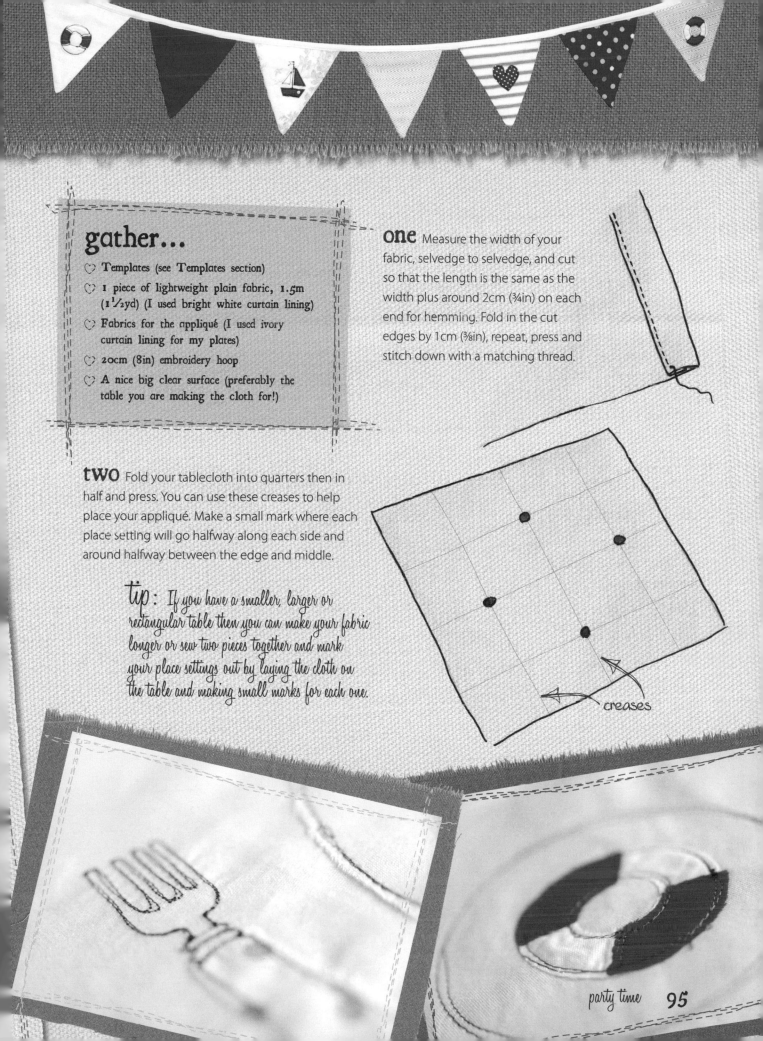

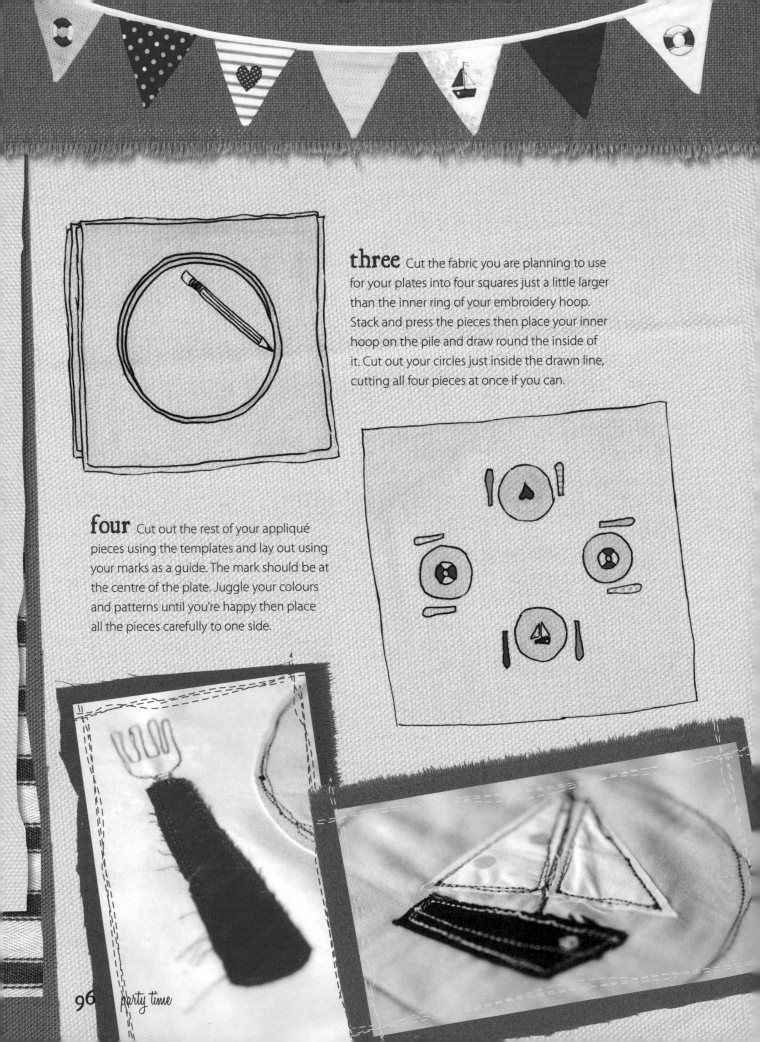

three Cut the fabric you are planning to use for your plates into four squares just a little larger than the inner ring of your embroidery hoop. Stack and press the pieces then place your inner hoop on the pile and draw round the inside of it. Cut out your circles just inside the drawn line, cutting all four pieces at once if you can.

four Cut out the rest of your appliqué pieces using the templates and lay out using your marks as a guide. The mark should be at the centre of the plate. Juggle your colours and patterns until you're happy then place all the pieces carefully to one side.

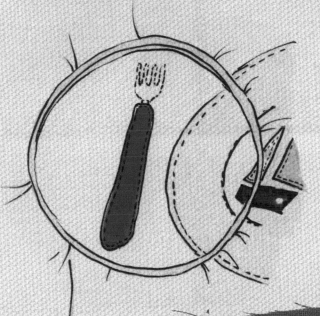

five Hoop up with your mark in the middle of the hoop. Stitch down all the pieces, starting with the outside of the plate (remembering that you can turn your hoop round if you can't quite get right to the edge), then the inner part of the plate, then moving the hoop to do each piece of cutlery.

six Trim your threads as neatly as you can on the back as this cloth is not backed so the reverse will show. You could of course back it with another piece of matching or contrasting fabric if desired. Press the whole cloth, pop over your table and get ready for those party guests to arrive!

tip: Be really careful not to get your base fabric folded under your hoop and accidentally sewn in and also watch out it doesn't drag through your cup of tea as you're working! (Yes, I do speak from experience!)

Happy Holidays

GROOVY GLASSES CASE

OH-SO-BRIGHT BOOKMARK

HAPPY HOLS WASH BAG

BEACH BEAUTIFUL BACKPACK

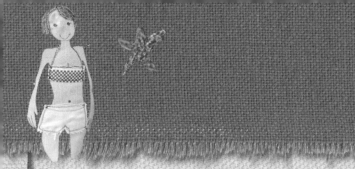

GROOVY
GLASSES CASE

difficulty rating: EASY PEASY

This is the perfect pouch for your specs on holiday. It's quite roomy so good for glasses or sunglasses and so bright you'll never struggle to find it in your bag! It's pretty simple to make but there is a little bit of magic in the pattern so trust me as you follow the steps!

here comes the sun...

This softly padded case offers plenty of protection.

gather...

- ♡ Templates (see Templates section)
- ♡ 1 piece of base fabric, 14 x 50cm (5½ x 20in)
- ♡ 1 piece of lining fabric, 14 x 50cm (5½ x 20in)
- ♡ 1 piece of backed wadding (batting), 14 x 50cm (5½ x 20in)
- ♡ Fabrics for the appliqué
- ♡ 1 piece of ribbon for the button loop, 12cm (4¾in) long
- ♡ Large bright button
- ♡ 10cm (4in) embroidery hoop
- ♡ Chopstick or other such pointy tool

one Fold and crease your base fabric 20cm (8in) from the right-hand end and 10cm (4in) from the left-hand end. Make small marks on the reverse at these crease points so you don't loose them. Your appliqué design will go on the middle section of your base fabric between these two creases. Do the same with your lining fabric.

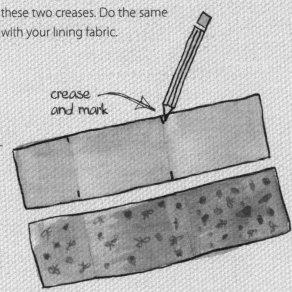

crease and mark

two Cut out your appliqué pieces using the templates. Hoop up and do your appliqué, stitching one eye at a time and moving the hoop to do the centre piece and the 'arms' of the glasses. I've used various thread colours in this design – grey for the drawing, white to stitch on the lenses and orange for the little star. Trim and press.

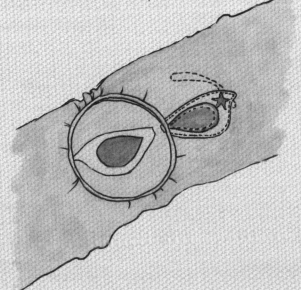

three Make a sandwich by laying your wadding (batting) down first, backed side down, then the base fabric and lining fabric right sides together (the base fabric lies on top of the wadding/batting).

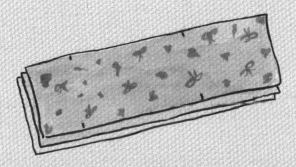

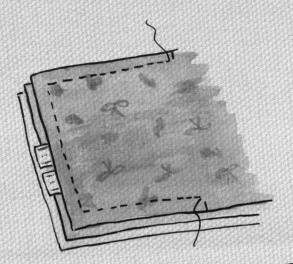

four With a 1cm (⅜in) seam allowance, stitch round the left-hand end of your sandwich starting at one mark and ending at the other. Insert your ribbon halfway along the end seam on the inside with the ends next to each other, not on top of each other.

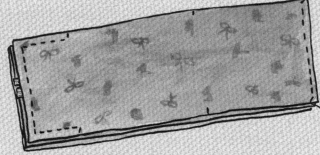

tip : Use a backed wadding (batting) for this design as it's much easier to run through a machine and keep stitched in place and won't go out of shape during washing or being squashed at the bottom of a handbag!

five Sew the far end of your sandwich together with a 1cm (⅜in) seam allowance. Then open out the sandwich lining up the far end seam with the seam you have sewn between the two marks. The wadding should always remain with the base fabric. Press to crease the new folds.

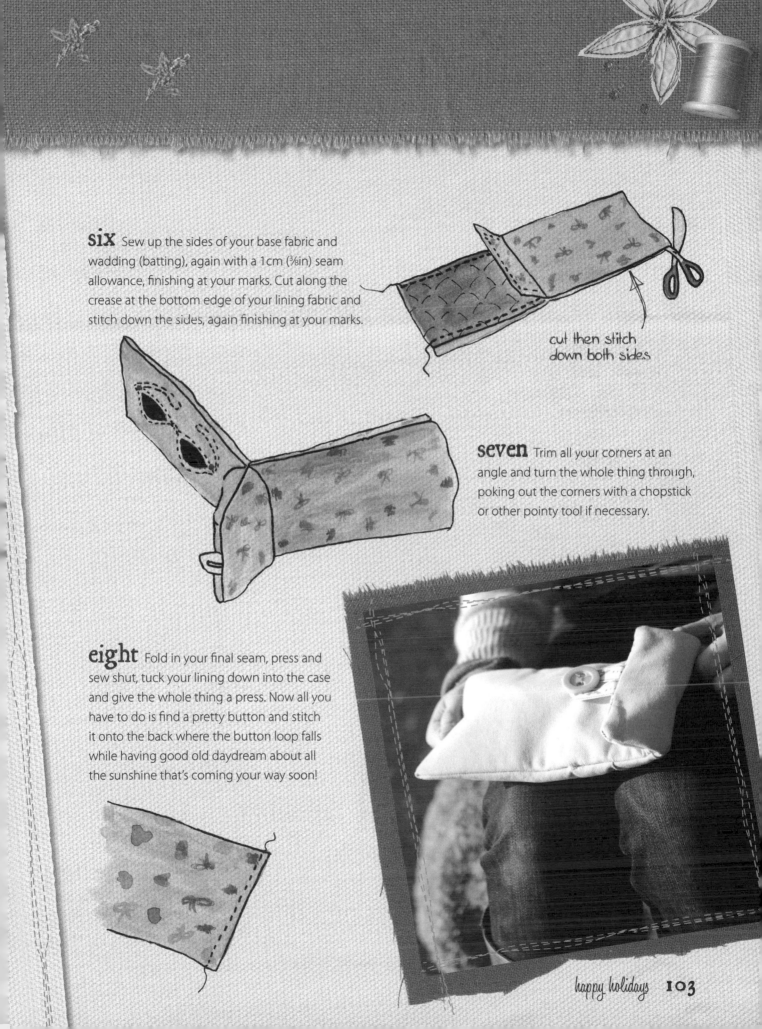

six Sew up the sides of your base fabric and wadding (batting), again with a 1cm (⅜in) seam allowance, finishing at your marks. Cut along the crease at the bottom edge of your lining fabric and stitch down the sides, again finishing at your marks.

cut then stitch
down both sides

seven Trim all your corners at an angle and turn the whole thing through, poking out the corners with a chopstick or other pointy tool if necessary.

eight Fold in your final seam, press and sew shut, tuck your lining down into the case and give the whole thing a press. Now all you have to do is find a pretty button and stitch it onto the back where the button loop falls while having good old daydream about all the sunshine that's coming your way soon!

OH-SO-BRIGHT BOOKMARK

difficulty rating: **EASY PEASY**

This colourful bookmark would make a lovely and useful present. You could use some of the other motifs in the book to add variation and make a little group of them for your book club friends. Or get creative and personalize the books in the design to reflect your own collection... hours of fun!

a pleasure to give or to keep...

With this pretty bookmark you'll never lose the thread of the story!

gather...

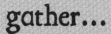

- ♡ Templates (see Templates section)
- ♡ 1 piece of fairly lightweight base fabric, 20 x 14cm (8 x 5½in)
- ♡ 1 piece of lightweight lining fabric, 20 x 14cm (8 x 5½in)
- ♡ 1 piece of narrow ribbon, 30cm (12in) long
- ♡ Fabrics for the appliqué
- ♡ 10cm (4in) embroidery hoop
- ♡ Chopstick or other such pointy tool

one Take your base fabric and draw around the template but don't cut it out just yet as it will be too small for your hoop. Cut out your appliqué pieces using the template and lay them out to see how it's looking.

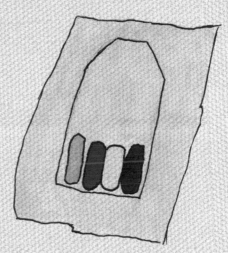

two Hoop up and stitch on your books, making sure you select a thread colour that will contrast well. Trim and press.

three Now you can cut out your base and lining fabrics as per the template. Once you've done that press up about 5mm (³⁄₁₆in) on the wide end of each piece, working on the reverse.

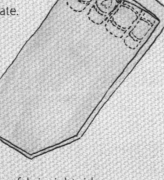

four Lay out your base fabric right side up, fold your ribbon in half and place it at the thin end so that it will be on the inside of the seam.

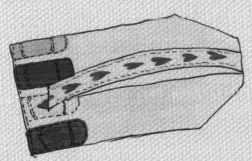

tip : As the appliqué pieces are quite small, you will need to get your fingers quite close to the needle to hold them in place while you stitch. If that's a bit scary, use the end of a pencil or little screwdriver (whatever's handy really) to hold them down.

five Place your lining fabric face down on top and pin if necessary. Stitch round with a 5mm (³⁄₁₆in) seam allowance leaving the folded edge open. Trim the corners and turn through, using a chopstick or other pointy tool if necessary to get everything nice and crisp. Then press.

six Sew your end seam shut using a matching thread then continue to stitch round about 2mm (¹⁄₁₆in) from the edge to give a decorative edge to your tag sewing a little reverse stitch at the start and finish. Now go and find a good book to read – oh hang on a minute you're already reading one!

HAPPY HOLS WASH BAG

difficulty rating: NOT TOO TRICKY

This jolly toiletries bag is the perfect thing for all those bathroomy bits and bobs that need to come on holiday with you. Line it with colourful waterproof fabric and you've got a practical and pretty travel companion ... just don't forget your tickets!

having a great time...wish you were here...

Appliqué and drawing with your machine are combined in this project.

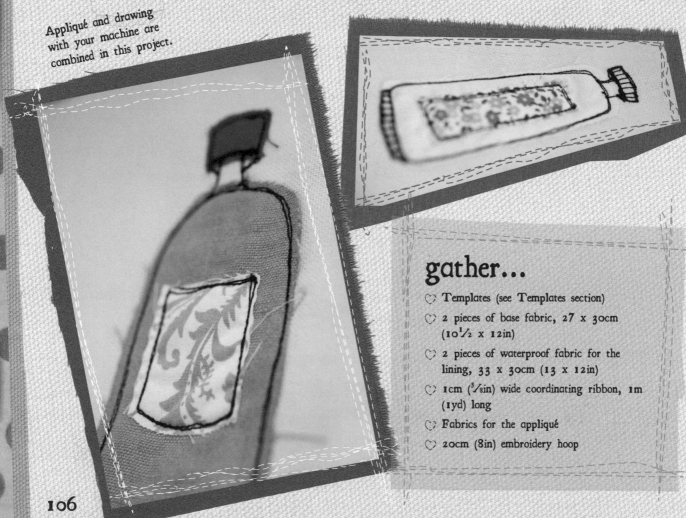

gather...

- ♡ Templates (see Templates section)
- ♡ 2 pieces of base fabric, 27 x 30cm (10½ x 12in)
- ♡ 2 pieces of waterproof fabric for the lining, 33 x 30cm (13 x 12in)
- ♡ 1cm (⅜in) wide coordinating ribbon, 1m (1yd) long
- ♡ Fabrics for the appliqué
- ♡ 20cm (8in) embroidery hoop

tip: As this design has quite
a bit of drawing in it around the
tops of the bottles, it might be an
idea to have a little practice first!

one Use the templates to cut out your pieces for the appliqué. Place them on one piece of your base fabric so you're happy with the composition, making small positioning marks underneath the pieces if necessary.

two Hoop up and do your appliqué and embroidery. You will need to move the hoop for each motif so work on one at a time and place your other pieces to one side. Move on to the next motif following your positioning mark (or do it by eye if you're feeling confident). Once you've sewn all the motifs, trim off all your thread ends and press.

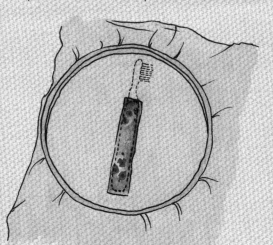

three Place one lining and one base piece of fabric right sides together and sew along the top edge with a 1.5cm (½in) seam allowance. Do the same for the other pair. Open out both pairs and iron the seams open and flat.

four Place the two pieces lining to lining, base to base, right sides together, lining the seams up and pinning if necessary. Stitch with a 1.5cm (½in) seam allowance from the right-hand corner of the lining round to the left-hand corner of the lining leaving the bottom edge of the lining open. Trim the corners at an angle and turn through.

tip: Put the waterproof fabric on the bottom and the outer fabric on the top as it will be easier to sew.

five Fold in the bottom seam of the lining and stitch shut using a matching thread and stitching close to the edge of the fabric.

six Tuck the lining into the base fabric leaving around 2.5cm (1in) poking out the top and press. Fold the excess piece of lining over onto the outside of the bag and sew down, tucking in the ribbon as you go. Make sure you leave a gap at the beginning and the end for the ribbon to come out through. You could use a contrasting top thread for this but use a bobbin that matches the colour of your lining fabric.

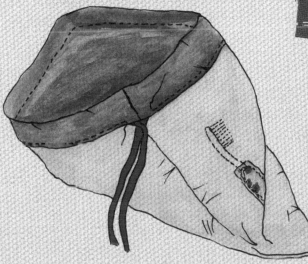

seven Tie the ends of your ribbon together to prevent them running through and so you can hang your bag up in your luxury hotel room on your lovely holiday … hmmmmm we can dream!

BEACH BEAUTIFUL BACKPACK

difficulty rating: **A BIT MORE TRICKY**

This is the ideal bag for a trip to the seaside or a day out sightseeing. Designed to be just the right size for the essentials but not so big you can't lift it, it has adjustable straps and an inside pocket, which frees up your hands for taking photos and drinking cocktails!

happy days down by the sea...

I still use the first backpack I made eight years ago on every holiday I go on.

gather...

- ♡ Templates (see Templates section)
- ♡ 3 pieces of medium- to heavyweight base fabric: Back 40 x 60cm (15¾ x 23½in); Front: 40cm (15¾in) square; Pocket: 30 x 20cm (12 x 8in)
- ♡ 3 pieces of medium-weight lining fabric (I used old-fashioned ticking), in the same sizes as the base fabric
- ♡ 2 pieces of medium-weight fabric for the straps, 12 x 110cm (4¾ x 43in)
- ♡ 4 pieces of 2.5cm (1in) wide webbing for the tabs and loops, 15cm (6in) long
- ♡ Fabrics for the appliqué
- ♡ Large button
- ♡ 20cm (8in) embroidery hoop
- ♡ Chopstick or other such pointy tool

one Cut out the appliqué pieces using the templates. Lay them out along the bottom edge of your front piece of base fabric until you are happy with the colour combinations. Then hoop up the beach huts one by one and stitch down. Trim and press.

three Stitch your straps as per the instructions for making handles in the Making up the projects section. They need to be around 3cm (1⅛in) wide when they're finished. As only one end of the each strap is sewn into the item (the other end is tied into the bottom loops), use the selvedge edge for the other end so that you don't have to hem them.

four Take the base and lining pieces for your pocket and place right sides together. Press up the bottom of each side by 1.5cm (½in) and pin the two pieces together. Stitch round with a 1.5cm (½in) seam allowance, leaving the folded edge open. Trim the corners off at an angle and turn through, poking out the corners with a chopstick or other pointy tool if necessary.

two Take the back piece of base fabric, fold down the top 20cm (8in) and press to crease. Cut along this crease and place to one side.

crease
and cut

tip: As this design is quite near the edge of the fabric, your fabric will not completely fill the hoop, so tighten the hoop a little more before you hoop up and really pull the fabric taut.

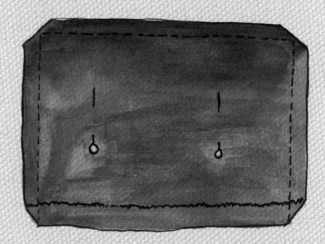

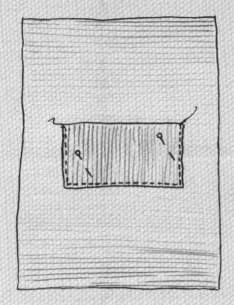

five Place your pocket piece with the folded open edge at the bottom around 28cm (11in) from the top of your back piece of lining. Make sure it's equidistant from each side and pin. Stitch your pocket down in a matching thread, starting with a small reverse stitch so it's nice and secure and stitching around 2mm (¹⁄₁₆in) from the edge. You will close the bottom seam of the pocket as you go.

tip: Using stripy fabric for the lining makes it much easier to get everything nice and straight!

six Place your back base fabric (the one without the appliqué) face up and position your straps and hanging loop at more or less the ¼, ½ and ¾ points along the top edge of the fabric. Make sure the ends of your hanging loop are next to each other rather than on top of each other.

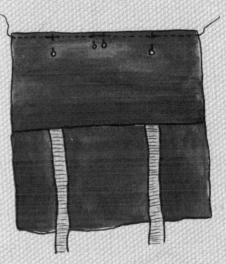

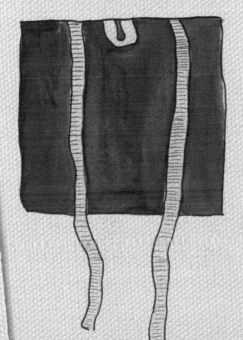

seven Lay your other back piece (the one you cut off earlier) face down in line with the top edge and pin everything in place. Stitch across with a 1.5cm (½in) seam allowance, reversing over the straps and hanging loop to make sure they are properly secured.

happy holidays **113**

eight Open out your back base fabric and lay it face up again with the straps pointing upwards then place two loops of webbing along the bottom edge at about the ¼ and ¾ points. Make sure the ends of your webbing are next to each other, not on top of each other.

nine Place your appliquéd front piece face down over this so the bottom edges line up and pin everything in place. Stitch across with a 1.5cm (½in) seam allowance, reversing over the loops so they are nice and secure.

ten Place your back base fabric face up again (this now consists of three pieces sewn together and is a bit long and unwieldy!) with the narrow piece at the top and bring the straps to the down position. Place your last loop halfway along the top edge with the ends next to each other, not on top of each other, as before. Place your back lining piece face down over this, top edges together and pin.

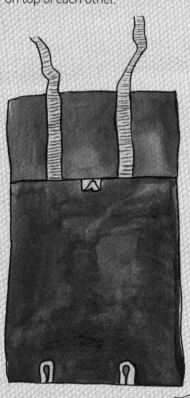

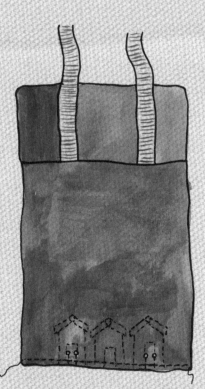

eleven Make two small marks on your lining in line with the first seam on your base fabric (the seam the straps are sewn into). With a 1.5cm (½in) seam allowance, sew round the top part, from the first mark to the second. You will sew the button loop in as you go – reverse over it to make sure it's nice and secure. Trim off your corners at an angle.

twelve Place your front piece of base fabric (the piece with the appliqué) right sides together with the front lining piece and stitch along the top edge with a 1.5cm (½in) seam allowance.

tip : *The next part is very similar to the tooth fairy pouch or the glasses case so if you've tried those projects already you're halfway there!*

fourteen Trim your corners and turn the whole thing through (you might need to get some strapping lads to help you!). Fold in your final seam and sew shut, keeping as close to the edge as you can. Poke the lining down into the bag, sew on a big button, tie your straps at a length that's nice and comfy, fill with swimsuit, book, camera and towel and get yourself down to the beach!

thirteen Place your whole piece on a flat surface and line it up so that the base fabric and lining fabric pieces line up lining to lining, base to base, right sides together. Pin at the points where the seams meet so they stay in line. Sew down the sides of your base fabric, stopping when you get to the point where the seams line up. Do the same with the lining pieces.

TEMPLATES

In most of the projects I have given measurements rather than templates for the base pieces of fabric. Those that need templates are included here, along with the appliqué templates. The appliqué works in layers to complete the whole motif so you will need to trace off the individual sections of the template (see Using the templates in the Making up the projects section).

TECHNIQUES

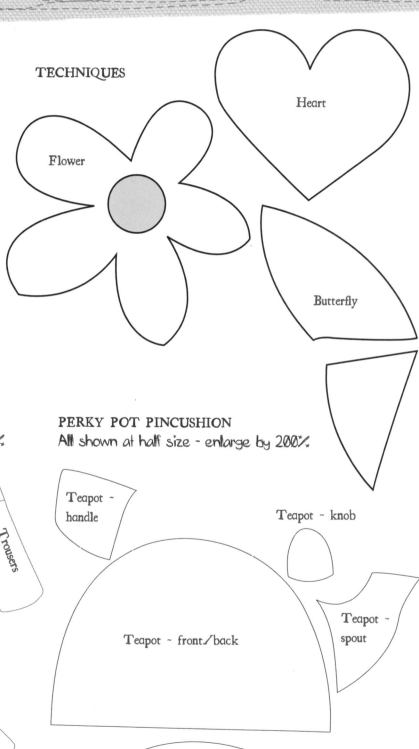

Flower

Heart

Butterfly

Getting Crafty

OH-SO-CRAFTY KNITTING BAG
All shown at half size - enlarge by 200%

Dress

Trousers

Top

PERKY POT PINCUSHION
All shown at half size - enlarge by 200%

Teapot ~ handle

Teapot ~ knob

Teapot ~ front/back

Teapot ~ spout

Teapot ~ bottom

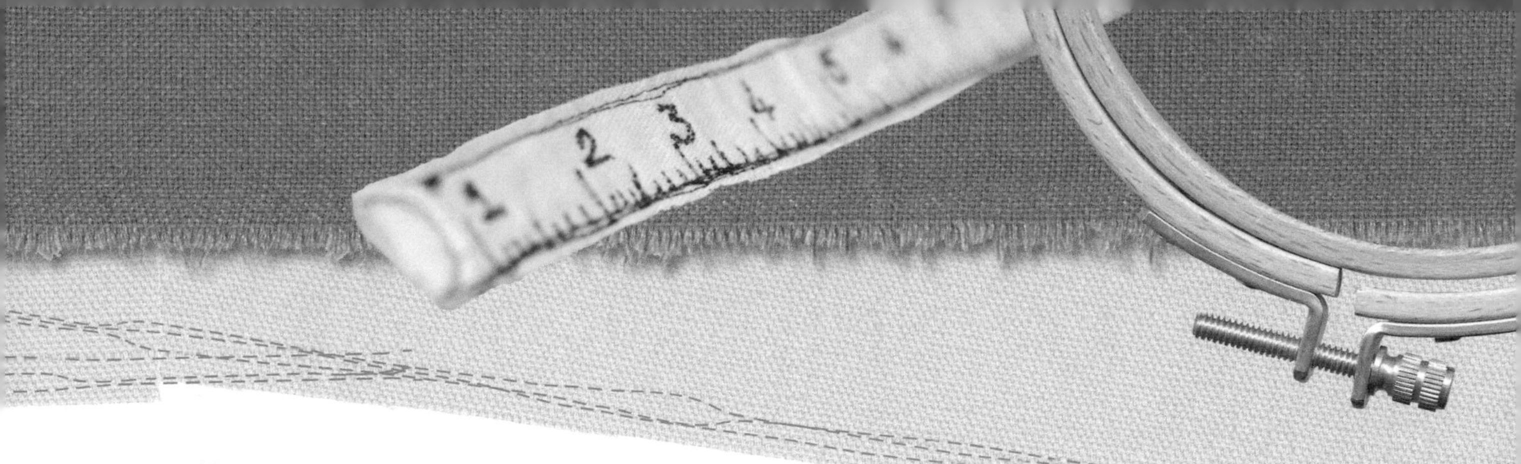

SEW FABULOUS SEWING KIT
Stitching guide shown in red

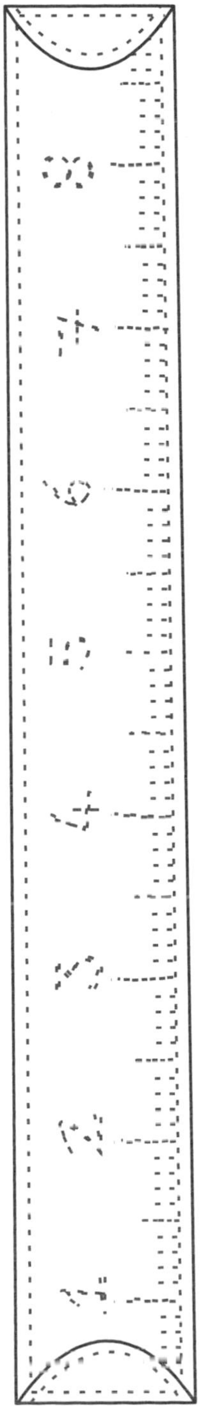

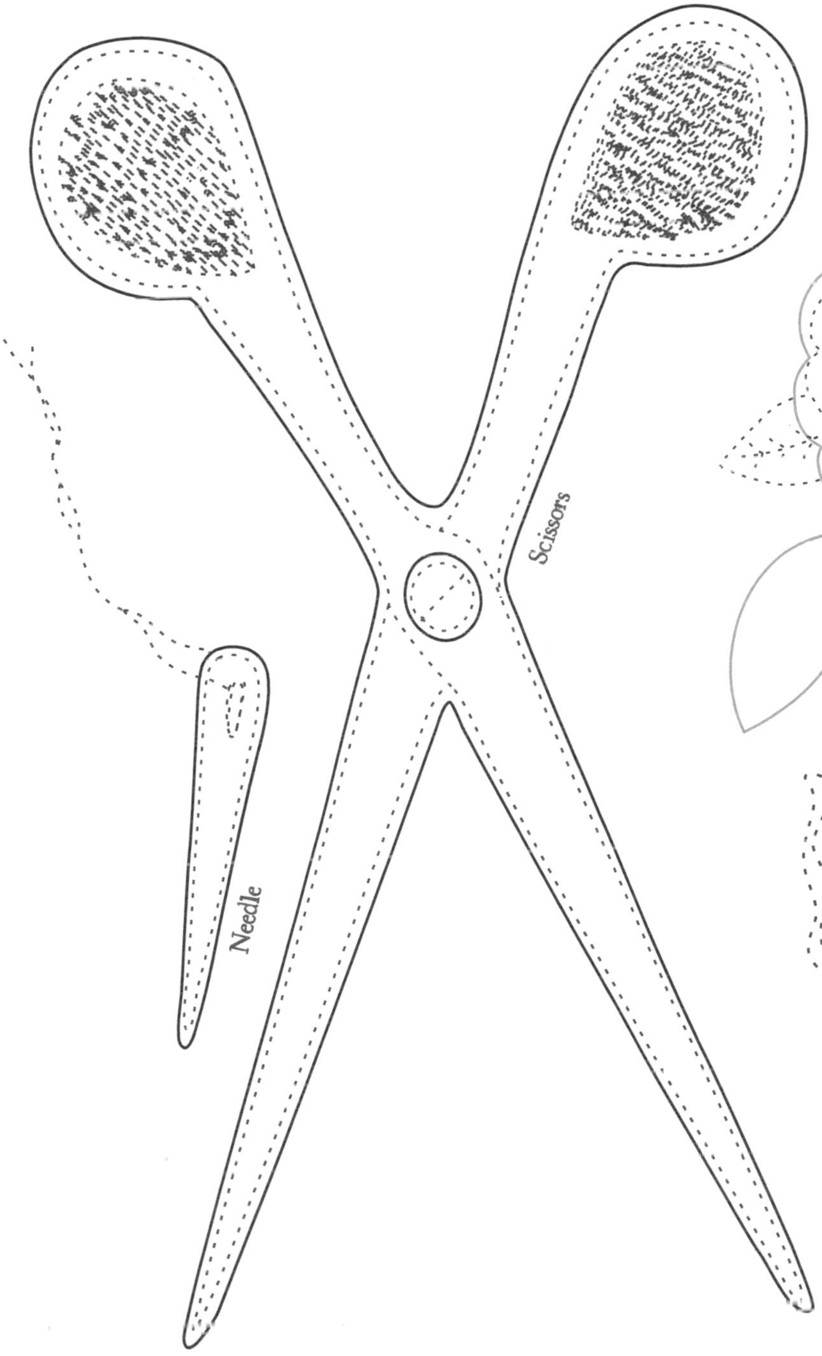

NIFTY NEEDLE CASE/PERKY POT PINCUSHION
Rose and leaf

cut two

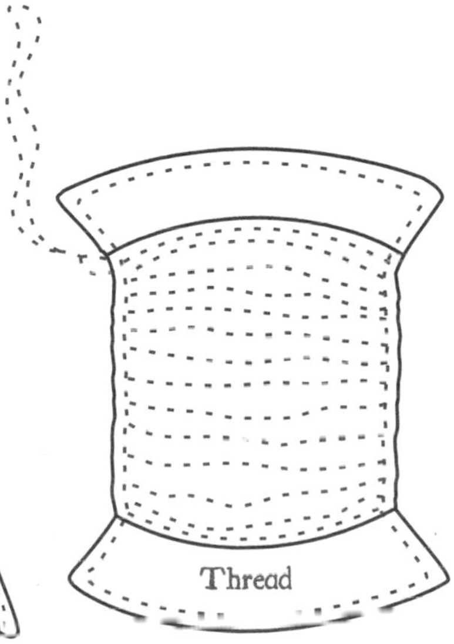

Scissors

Needle

Thread

Ruler

New Arrivals

TOOTH FAIRY PILLOW POUCH

Fairy

BONNY BABY BIB

Apple and leaves – use the motifs
from Summer Fruits Baby Blanket
cut one apple and two leaves

Bib
cut one base
and one lining

Stitching guide

NURSERY TOYS WALL ART
All shown at half size - enlarge by 200%

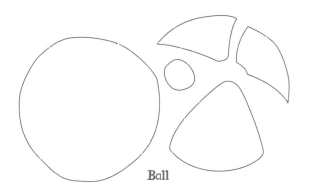

Ball

Duck with stitching guide

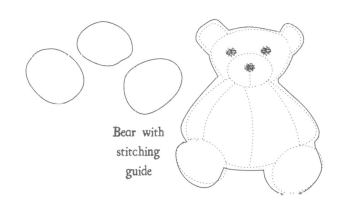

Bear with
stitching
guide

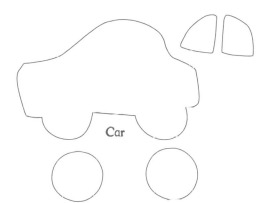

Car

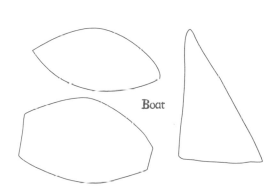

Boat

SUMMER FRUITS BABY BLANKET
All shown at half size - enlarge by 200%

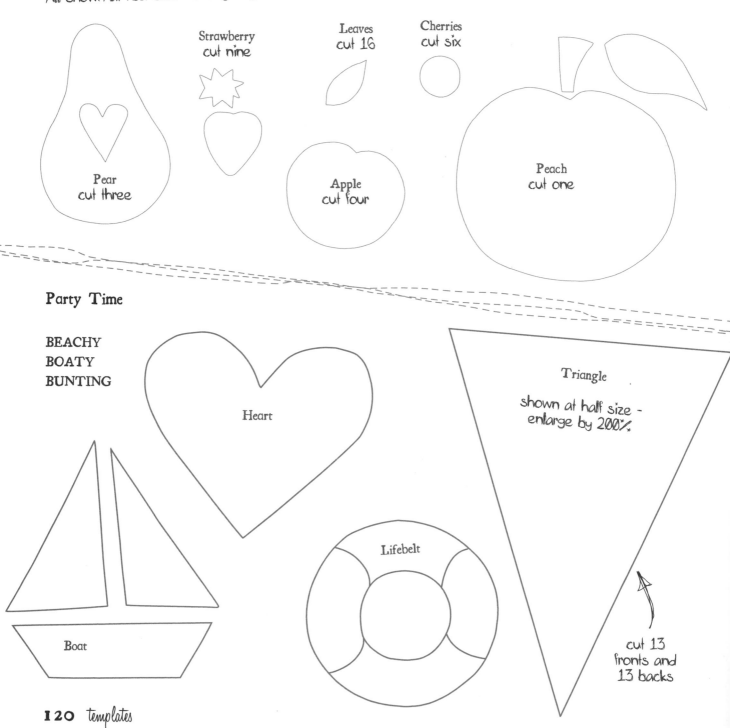

Strawberry
cut nine

Leaves
cut 16

Cherries
cut six

Pear
cut three

Apple
cut four

Peach
cut one

Party Time

BEACHY BOATY BUNTING

Heart

Triangle

shown at half size -
enlarge by 200%

Boat

Lifebelt

cut 13
fronts and
13 backs

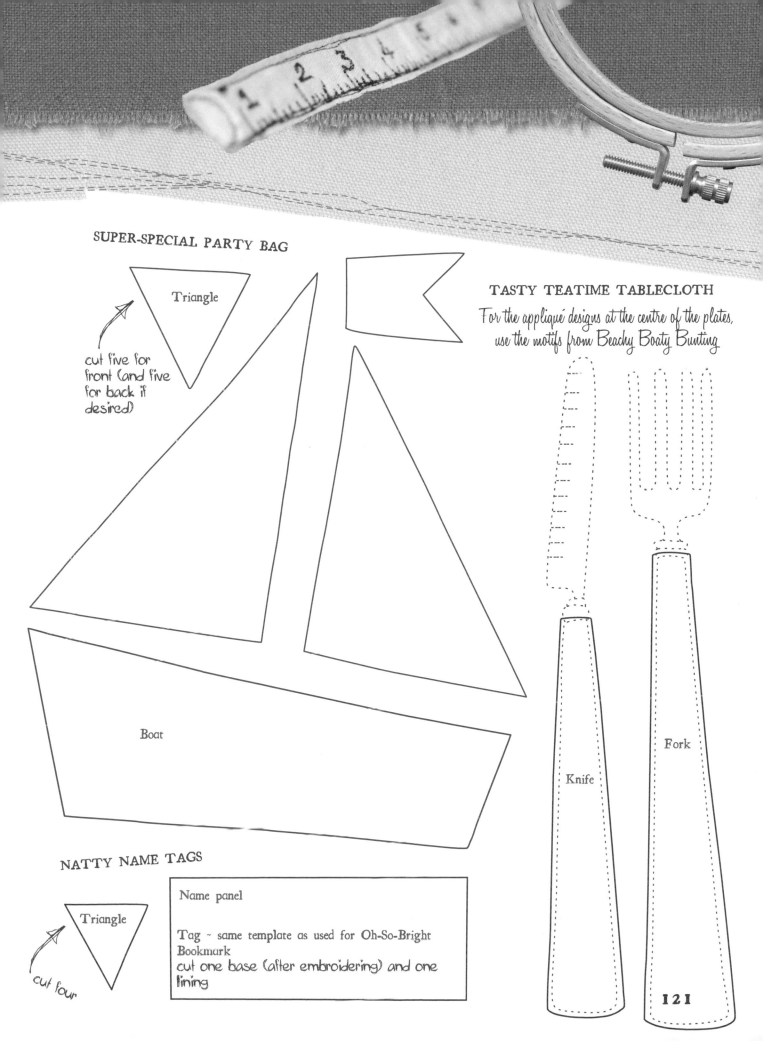

SUPER-SPECIAL PARTY BAG

Triangle

cut five for front (and five for back if desired)

Boat

TASTY TEATIME TABLECLOTH

For the appliqué designs at the centre of the plates, use the motifs from Beachy Boaty Bunting

Knife

Fork

NATTY NAME TAGS

Triangle

cut four

Name panel

Tag ~ same template as used for Oh-So-Bright Bookmark
cut one base (after embroidering) and one lining

121

Happy Holidays

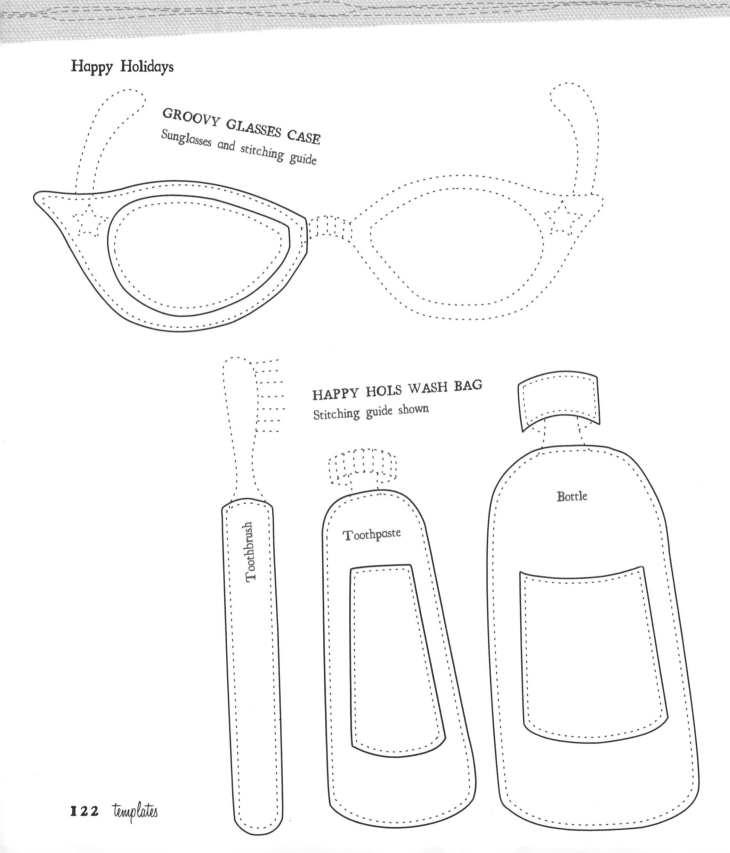

GROOVY GLASSES CASE
Sunglasses and stitching guide

HAPPY HOLS WASH BAG
Stitching guide shown

Toothbrush

Toothpaste

Bottle

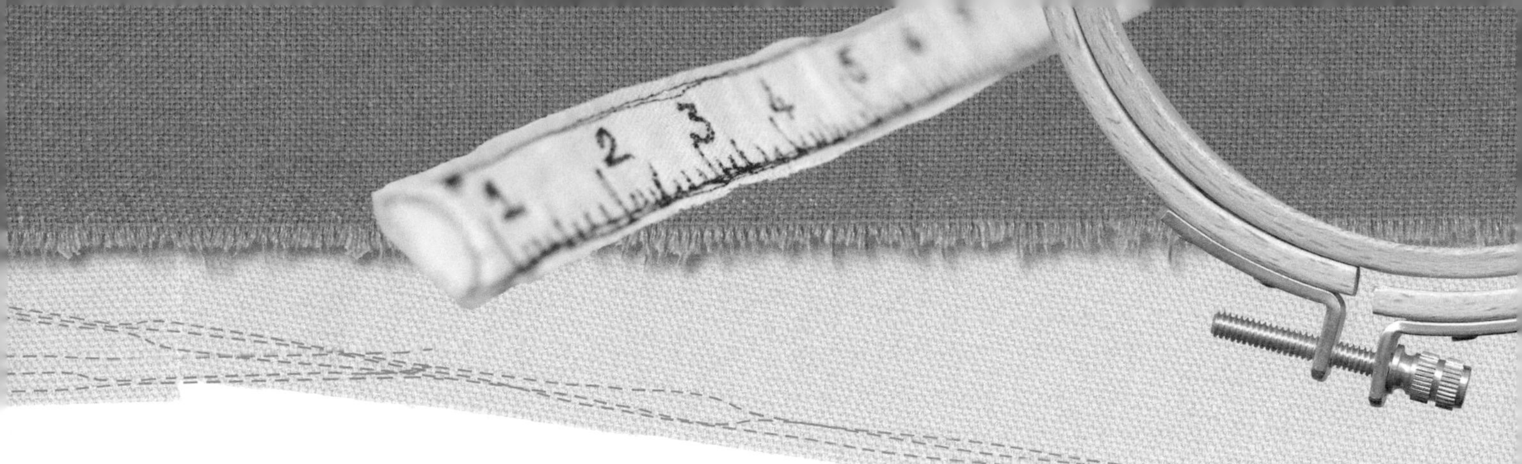

BEACH BEAUTIFUL BACKPACK

Beach hut

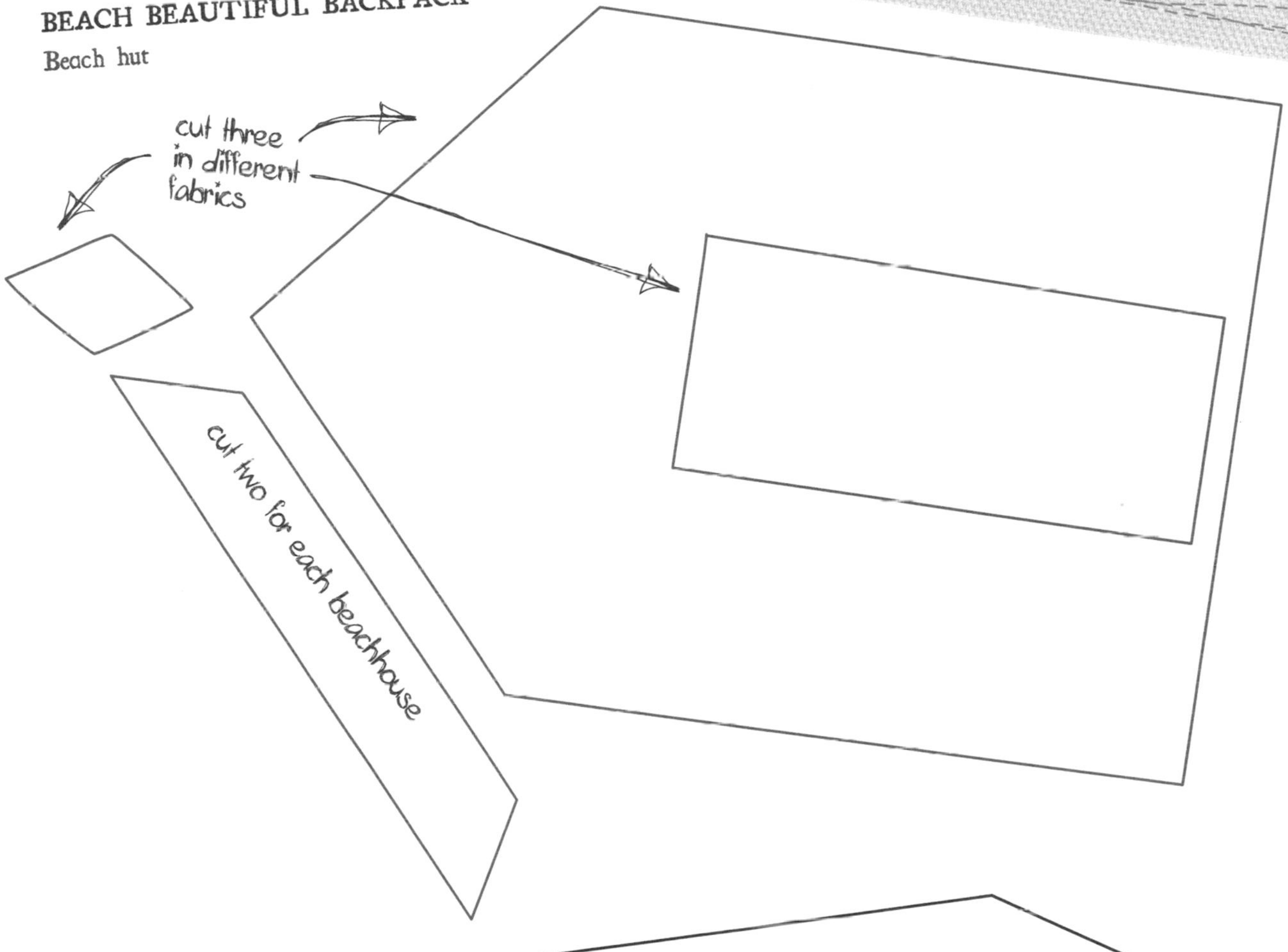

cut three
in different
fabrics

cut two for each beachhouse

OH-SO-BRIGHT BOOKMARK

Tag - cut one base (after
embroidering) and one lining

Books and Stitching guide

Suppliers

Here are some ideas for reliable suppliers of fabric, thread, trimmings and tools, but you will also find that your local vintage and thrift stores are great places to scavenge for the most gorgeous old fabrics, buttons and trimmings.

BASED IN THE USA

For great fabrics in Manhattan
Mood Fabrics
225 West 37th St, New York
NY 10018
Tel: 212-730-5003
www.moodfabrics.com

Endless floors of gorgeous fabric
Britex Fabrics
146 Geary St, San Francisco
CA 94108
Tel: 415-392-2910
www.britexfabrics.com

Great for discount fabrics
www.fabric.com

Great all-round fabric supplier
JoAnn Fabrics
www.joann.com

Great for chintz, dots and stripes
www.reprodepot.com

BASED IN CANADA

For fabrics and notions
Hamels Fabrics & Quilting
5843 Lickman Rd,
Chilliwack, B.C. V2R 4B5
Tel: 604-846-4350
www.hamelsfabrics.com

For threads, embroidery hoops, needles and accessories
P and G Enterprises
Rolly View, Alberta, T0C 2K0
Tel: 780-986-8931
www.pandgenterprises.com

For general sewing notions
Joanne's Creative Notions
Tel: 905-453-1805
www.joannescreativenotions.com

BASED IN THE UK

For embroidery hoops, threads, ribbons and more
www.poppytreffry.co.uk

For great fabrics, buttons, trimmings
Truro Fabrics
Lemon Quay, Truro,
Cornwall TR1 2LW
Tel: 01872 222130
www.shop.trurofabrics.com

For lovely furnishing fabrics
Cotton Mills
Peoples Palace, Pydar St, Truro,
Cornwall TR1 2AZ
Tel: 01872 278545

For a stunning range of threads
Calico Laine
16 Liscard Crescent, Liscard,
Wirral CH44 1AE
Tel: 0151 336 3939
www.calicolaine.co.uk

For a massive range of trimmings
Barnett Lawson Trimmings Ltd
16–17 Little Portland St,
London W1W 8NE
Tel: 0207 636 8591
www.bltrimmings.com

For quality embroidery hoops
Tandem Cottage Needlework Ltd
PO Box 40, Glossop,
Derbyshire SK13 1FB
Tel: 01457 862610
www.tandem-cottage.co.uk

For scissors and other equipment
Morplan
56 Great Titchfield St,
London W1W 7DF
Tel: 0207 636 1887
www.morplan.com

BASED IN AUSTRALIA

For vintage, retro and organic fabrics, fabric bundles, trimmings and notions
Funky Fabrix
Shop 4/12 Blackwood St, Mitchelton,
Queensland 4503
Tel: 0435 012356
www.funkyfabrix.com.au

For gorgeous designer fabrics
I Just Love That Fabric
Tel: 5534 8160
www.ijustlovethatfabric.com.au

Contemporary fabrics and notions with loads of inspiration and a blog
Kelani Fabrics
Tel: 9438 4145
www.kelanifabric.com.au

BASED IN NEW ZEALAND

For lovely fabrics on the south island
Timaru Sewing Centre
173 Stafford St, Timaru 7910
Tel: 03-688-6764
www.timarusewing.co.nz

For sewing machines and accessories
Itch to Stitch
22 John St, Whangarei, Northland
www.itchtostitch.co.nz

For great value fabrics in Wellington
The Fabric Warehouse
126 Hutt Rd, Kaiwharawhara,
Wellington 6035
Tel: 04-473-8150
thefabricwarehouse@xtra.co.nz

Fabric stores in Auckland, Wellington, Christchurch and Dunedin
Global Fabrics
www.globalfabrics.co.nz

Sources of Inspiration

Inspiration is all around us – and can sometimes be found in the most surprising of places. The list below shows just a few of the things that have inspired me along the way. I hope you find them interesting too.

SHOPS

Anthropologie – across the US and UK
This American chain has now landed in London too. I've loved it ever since first visiting in San Francisco years ago and I now make an annual pilgrimage to their store in New York. Exquisite styling and beautiful clothes and, my personal favourite, gorgeous mix-and-match ceramics.
www.anthropologie.com

Illustrated Living – Truro
A lot closer to my home this shop carries some amazing designers like Mini Moderns, Orla Kiely, Lush and Donna Wilson. I love the crisp display and the slightly 50s slant on things. They have a great website too.
www.illustratedliving.co.uk

BLOGS

From Britain With Love
This ever-so-pretty website and blog features the latest in design, craft, food, drink and plenty more all from Britain. Their newsletter is a great way of keeping in touch with what's going on in British design and I like their features on different businesses. They have lots of great competitions too.
www.frombritainwithlove.com

Print and Pattern
This blog is all about pattern and is just awash with inspiring colour combinations and ideas. It's also been made into a book which I was lucky enough to receive for my birthday – I love it!
www.printpattern.blogspot.com

BOOKS

Julie Arkell: *Home*
I've had this book for a long time but it never fails to inspire me. The photos of her workspace are so amazing and her eccentric creations are very much one offs.
ISBN-10: 1-9009-4178-3
ISBN-13: 978-1-9009-4178-5

Sarah Midda: *In and Out of the Garden*
This pretty little book has also been on my shelf for many years. The detailed watercolour illustrations are so sweet and whimsical, they make me want to do my own storybooks.
ISBN-10: 0-8948-0193-7
ISBN-13: 978-0-8948-0193-8

MAGAZINES

Selvedge
This lovely square-shaped magazine is full of fascinating articles and sumptuous photography. Even the adverts (for things like rug-making in Rajasthan) are gorgeous.
www.selvedge.org

Mollie Makes
This is my newest love. It's choc full of gorgeous photography and inspiring articles about making, buying and selling craft. And there's always a very cute free gift too!
www.molliemakes.makingspot.com

PLACES

The V&A – London
This huge museum is a never-ending source of ideas and inspiration and its store carries a really strong collection of designers. I love the jewellery rooms and the Korean galleries.
www.vam.ac.uk

The Pitt Rivers Museum – Oxford
This anthropological museum in historic Oxford contains a vast collection of everyday objects from hair combs to armour. Everything is packed into old glass cases and drawers. You could lose yourself in there for hours.
www.prm.ox.ac.uk

EVENTS

The Contemporary Craft Festival – Bovey Tracey, UK
A fantastic selection of British Crafts (including our good selves!) with over 150 exhibitors as well as food, drink, a big kids tent, workshops and street theatre.
www.craftsatboveytracey.co.uk

About the Author

Poppy Treffry runs a busy textile design company based in Cornwall, England. Her range of quirky accessories for fashion and the home sells in department stores and boutiques throughout the UK, USA, Japan and Europe.

Poppy had produced bespoke collections for the famous Fortnum & Mason department store in London and the wonderful Bettys Tea Rooms in Yorkshire. She has also produced printed products for the cult US retailer Anthropologie.

Poppy lives in Penzance with her partner, jeweller Justin Duance, and daughter Biba who has already got her first sewing machine and has made her first dolly dress (she'll be put to work very soon!). This is her second book.

For more information on Poppy's products and courses, as well as online shopping visit www.poppytreffry.co.uk

Acknowledgments

I'd like to thank the whole team at Poppy Treffry – Faye, Sara, Freya, Briony, Danny, Becky and Kim for making everything run so smoothly while I got my head down and wrote this book. I'd also like to thank Justin for being so supportive and keeping food on the table and wine in the fridge! And Biba for just being gorgeous!

Index

A DAVID & CHARLES BOOK
© F&W Media International, Ltd 2012

David & Charles is an imprint of F&W Media International, Ltd
Brunel House, Forde Close, Newton Abbot, TQ12 4PU, UK

F&W Media International, Ltd is a subsidiary of F+W Media, Inc
10151 Carver Road, Cincinnati OH45242, USA

Text and Designs © Poppy Treffry 2012
Layout and Photography © F&W Media International, Ltd 2012

First published in the UK and USA in 2012

ISBN-13: 978-1-4463-0186-9 paperback
ISBN-10: 1-4463-0186-9 paperback

Paperback edition printed in China by RR Donnelley for:
F&W Media International, Ltd
Brunel House, Forde Close, Newton Abbot, TQ12 4PU, UK

10 9 8 7 6 5 4 3 2

Acquisitions Editor: **Sarah Callard**
Editor: **James Brooks**
Project Editor: **Ame Verso**
Art Editor: **Sarah Underhill**
Photographers: **Lorna Yabsley and Jack Kirby**
Senior Production **Controller: Kelly Smith**

F+W Media publishes high quality books on a wide range of subjects.
For more great book ideas visit: **www.stitchcraftcreate.co.uk**